# DOWN FROM ABOVE, UP FROM BELOW

## WORKING WITH LORD PENTLAND AND THE GURDJIEFF IDEAS

Jane Madeline Gold

# DOWN
# FROM ABOVE,
# UP
# FROM BELOW

## WORKING WITH LORD PENTLAND
## AND THE GURDJIEFF IDEAS

Jane Madeline Gold

# TABLE OF CONTENTS

Introduction  *ix*

Note to the Reader  *xiv*

Preface  *xv*


PART ONE — THE OFFICE


The Lost Pages and Sustained Effort  *3*

At the Office  *5*

Awareness and Sensation  *8*

Centers  *10*

A Brilliant and Clever Mind  *13*

Hard Tasks, Extraordinary Outcomes  *15*

The Books  *20*

Humor  *23*

Fritz Peters  *25*


PART TWO — DOWN FROM ABOVE


The Miraculous  *31*

"If You Work Consciously,
Conscious Spirits Will Be Sent to Guide You"  35

What will change the world?  38

On Sorrow and Joy  40

Higher Octaves of Communication  43

The Most Unusual Experience  45

Intimations of a Higher World  46

God and Mammon  51

The Ray of Creation  60

Fated Encounters  61

More Lessons  64

Trust in the Process of Your Life  69

On the Work Being Called "the Work," God,
and the Difficulty of Language  72

The Best Karma  74

An Encounter with Krishnamurti  76

PART THREE – UP FROM BELOW

The Psychological Teaching of George Gurdjieff  83

Psychology and Subjectivity  87

Inner Considering  93

On Love  96

What Is the Nature of Identification?  99

My Relationship with Lord Pentland  *102*

Chief Feature  *105*

It is a Blessing to be Born Into a Bloodline Where
There Are Things To Be Worked Out  *108*

Duly Chastened  *111*

Traveling with Lord Pentland  *115*

Shamanism/Dreamtime  *117*

On the Institutionalization/Hierarchy-
Heirophants-Heirophant-asses  *120*

Life Is the Great Teacher  *124*

Behind Me  *126*

EPILOGUE  *129*

ACKNOWLEDGMENTS  *131*

BIBLIOGRAPHY/READING LIST  *132*

*This is the Cooper's Hawk that showed up in the palm tree*
*outside my office at the moment I first sat down to write this*
*book in earnest and made my wish for its good outcome.*

# INTRODUCTION

When I was 17 years old my father died and, with that devastating passing, my disappointment in life – not only my subjective life, the whole life of the world around me – became pervasive and troubling. I began a search for answers, for ideas, and for a teaching that would help me to understand and explore the big questions. For as long as I could remember, I had had an acute interest in our mortality. It didn't make sense to me that we would live and die randomly in an accidentally created world in such a beautiful, intricate and mysterious universe. There was obviously an implicit and intelligent order in the natural world that didn't seem to exist in the conditions of life that humanity created. There had to be something else.

For readers who are unfamiliar with him, in the early part of the twentieth century there appeared in Europe a man named George Gurdjieff who brought to the West a synthesis of ageless wisdom, physical and cosmic laws, a comprehensive human psychology, a path toward wakefulness and against somnambulism and hypnosis, and a way to inner freedom, conscience and consciousness.

Prior to his death, Gurdjieff appointed Henry John Sinclair, Baron Pentland of Lyth, more commonly known as Lord Pentland, to lead this Work in the United States. The title was inherited from his father who had been a Scottish politician and had served as the Governor of Madras. Lord Pentland was a remarkable human being, an electrical engineer and businessman by profession, extraordinary in *being*, intellect and appearance.

My life intersected with his; I became his personal secretary in New York for three and a half years. The story of how this came about appears as the Preface to this book, a reprint of an article I wrote in 2001. This article attracted the attention of other students, who urged me to continue to write.

Then again, there was Lord Pentland's query: "Will you write about me after I die?"

During the entire time I knew him and after serving in his employ, he never stopped teaching me. His work and love have momentum beyond his parting.

For students of Lord Pentland, his passing was a grievous loss. It is possible only now for me to remember the full impact of who had been in our midst and how generous he had been with his knowledge and wisdom. It is my primary intent to remember him here with love. For it is love, more than any idea, that has the potential to transform.

———

When I was four years old and recuperating from a serious surgery, standing in front of a white dresser with a lamb decal on it, I had the thought, "The earth is a speck of dust on the fingernail of God."

In my late teens, first learning to sit with myself, or meditate, I had a spontaneous memory of being six months old in a crib. I could see a sliver of light coming through the doorway. I was angry, very angry, thinking, "Just bring me the damn bottle." Though this is obviously a preverbal age, it isn't pre-emotional: infants are keenly aware and have a range of strong emotions. I later found out that the bottle had in fact been withheld for long periods of time and that the bottle that was given was propped up on pillows for me to drink from.

These two early memories elucidate the dual nature of our experience: cosmological and psychological. *Above and Below.*

And then I began in earnest a search for a teaching that would help me to understand the two aspects of that reality. Because it was clear to me, from early on, that I inhabited something vast, but also that I was in a true psychological bind.

I was then fortunate, at nineteen, to find the teachings of George Gurdjieff. And not long thereafter to come into the employ of Lord Pentland.

As noted above, George Gurdjieff was a Greek-Armenian who, in the early part of the twentieth century, laid out and brought to the West a comprehensive spiritual (and cosmological) teaching side by side with a psychological one, based, it is understood, on his studies and wide travels in the East. The teaching is non-denominational, universal, and perennial in its scope. One could say that Gurdjieff's main premise is that human beings are asleep, but have the possibility of awakening. Possibilities of not only awakening to and in this life, but experiencing levels of consciousness beyond the ordinary. Of this he says, "Man's possibilities are very great."

Moreover, Gurdjieff suggests, human beings have the potential to develop and mature psychologically. But if we develop in only one of the two aspects – spiritual or psychological – our development will be lopsided and inharmonious.

In my view, his psychological teaching has so far

received too little attention, although the teaching insists that our psychological lives are important. They are not only the scaffolding for spiritual work, they are in and of themselves meaningful. As Gurdjieff says, "It is a blessing to be born into a bloodline where there are things to be worked out."

———————

The title phrase, *Down from Above*, refers to the movement of the Higher down into us, from Above. This we might attract through our sincerity, faith, past actions, and other factors both known and unknown to us. *Up from Below* refers to our own efforts to reach toward what is Above from our human being and psychology. As Gurdjieff elucidates, it is the lower functions that are not functioning properly and it is our task, should we understand and accept it, to bring our human functions into harmonious development. In my experience, there is a correlation between these two, that is, the more I consciously suffer, or enter into the lower, the more I might know the higher in myself.

The teaching is so vast that one lifetime does not render adequate time to work with and understand its multiplicity of ideas. In these pages I explore the ideas that have touched me. But this is far from a scholarly study of the teachings; many such are available elsewhere.

How I came to work for Lord Pentland can, I feel, best be described as the work of *karma*, or the mystical force of Great Nature which brings people together for its own hidden purposes.

Lord Pentland was a phenomenally interesting man. He

exuded a gravitas that commanded respect and he looked like no one else on earth. He was brilliant, committed, and sincere. Of his detractions, I say nothing. That he was human, and therefore erred, should be obvious.

Some of my stories take place in the realm of the numinous. Many may find these incredulous. It is an unfortunate tendency of some who do not understand a thing to say that it is the product of imagination, wishful thinking or mere neuronal activity. But bear in mind that Gurdjieff speaks to the higher octaves of our functioning; these are real, not imagined, and always operating. Put in other words, we can see, experience and understand on multiple levels and with multiple organs, not just our eyes and ears.

We do not presently have tools to measure transcendent phenomena, those things that do not appear easily to the senses. But what P. D. Ouspensky (one of Gurdjieff's early students) in *In Search of the Miraculous* refers to as *facts* are part of my story.

There is a reality that can, in fact, be apprehended as miraculous and that exists objectively. In this narrative, I hope that I am able to communicate some sense of that mysterious beauty and intelligence.

## NOTE TO THE READER

I have written this story for my brothers and sisters, those also drawn by magnetic force to these extraordinary teachings and to Lord Pentland. I hope it renders the feeling of the man to those who knew him and to those who did not. This is for the reader then, and my hope is that it evokes some measure of feeling. Without feeling, we are barely human.

I also hope that you can forgive the narcissism within. I hope it is not too bad. I can only promise to do the same in return. There is pathological, malignant narcissism, and there is healthy narcissism, what Gurdjieff refers to as "conscious egoism." My wish is that this is, among other things, a story about the right kind of Self-Love, not the wrong kind.

Further, although it doesn't seem to be much practiced, if at all, the exercise that Gurdjieff gives to Ouspensky's group in *In Search of the Miraculous*, that is, to tell one's life story to the group, seems to apply. I seriously recommend telling your life story: it is a powerful experience.

## Working with Lord Pentland
### (First Published in *Stopinder*, Summer 2001)

I worked for Lord Pentland at American British Electric Company at Rockefeller Plaza in New York City for three and one-half years in the early seventies. Lord Pentland was the president of the Gurdjieff Foundation in New York. He was appointed by George Gurdjieff to head up his work in America. During the time I worked for him, he published The First Series, *All and Everything: Beelzebub's Tales To His Grandson* in paperback; *Views From the Real World*; and the Third Series, *Life Is Real Only Then When "I Am."* It was a profoundly prolific time, in terms of the literary output as well as the many people who came to meet with Lord Pentland in his office to seek the Work. We call the "Work" those methods put forth by Gurdjieff intended to harmonize and develop our lower functions as well as bring us into contact with our higher natures, our God particle, if you will, or cosmic consciousness.

Lord Pentland was eager for students who could absorb his teaching, which he had brought forth in himself to remarkable levels of perception. Indeed, he taught all the time, whether by his own presence – I myself saw that he had eyes all over his body – or through his words or actions. He pleaded with me, "Use me. Use me." And so I tried to come to work every day with my attention directed toward him, as well as on myself, and also to the work at hand.

A good part of the discourse with Lord Pentland was

about the miraculous, higher states of consciousness, and life after death. But he was not only about higher states. He was a brilliant psychologist, if not trained as one, who knew how to provide conditions and combine people for seeing and development.

*Self-remembering* forms the cornerstone of both the psychological and cosmological teachings in the Gurdjieff Work. Whether I see myself in an undeveloped essential part, or at the place where the Higher descends in me, that is a point of self-remembering. If I fail to remember myself, I am less likely to see or hear an aspect of the Higher or its intermediaries. And if, as Gurdjieff says, a man or woman works consciously, conscious spirits will be sent to guide him or her, it becomes imperative for me to remember myself if I seek help from Above.

A few years before he died in 1984, Lord Pentland invited me to meet with him in California, where I was now living. He dictated some notes on a talk he was to give at Esalen on the Art of Living. He asked for my comments and I gave him my impressions. Then he startled me by asking, "Will you write about me after I die?" I was too stunned to reply first because, naively, I refused to consider his death, but also because I did not then, nor did I for years, consider that I could do justice to the man by writing about him. Shortly before he died, he encouraged me by saying, "Take responsibility for what you know." Then, a year after his death, all the things he said came rolling out from my memory, as though released from a reel, such that I always carried paper with me, ready to record impressions as they appeared. This went on for three months and stopped as abruptly as it began. As I worked with this material for another fifteen years, I realized that he put this task *in* me, and also that I had accepted it.

I understood John Pentland to be a man who struggled with all the things that made him mortal, in addition to the pursuit of self-transformation. It is precisely this that made him an exquisite human being. A tall ectomorph, at once severe and loving, he suffered like the rest of us. As far as I could determine, he had the best intentions in dealing with his students. He created conditions in which we were forced to see ourselves, and often it was a bitter pill. He admitted to his errors, at least to me.

In 1971, I had been living in California, and Lord Pentland invited me to visit him in New York. I had begun the Work there in 1968 under the aegis of Christopher Fremantle, also a remarkable man, an artist, gentle and kind. When I got to New York, Lord Pentland asked me to come to his home on Independence Avenue in Riverdale at 6 a.m. and from there we would drive together to Armonk, the Workhouse in upstate New York. He instructed me to take only buses and trains – no taxis – which meant I would have to travel through Harlem and the Bronx in the dark, by myself. I was a young woman and, at the time, quite small. I took on the task in spite of considerable fear.

I got to Riverdale without incident, though I ran into some people on the train whose presence concerned me. I stayed focused throughout on my intention. Then we were in Lord Pentland's car, a short distance from his house, and stopped at a stop sign, when a rough-looking street person saw me light a cigarette and knocked at my window, asking for a smoke. I reached into my bag to give him a cigarette. "Don't give it to him," Pentland said. I considered his comment, and decided to give the man a cigarette. "Don't give it to him," Pentland said again. I decided I am giving the man a cigarette no matter what Pentland says and, as I do so, he said, "OK, give it to him." I already know that blind obedience is not what is required.

Later that same day, I am sitting in a row at the rear, struggling to stay awake during the reading that ends the day. Lord Pentland is reading. Suddenly, I come to with alertness. I know with certainty that he is reading to me, even though there are no outward signs. He is reading a talk of Gurdjieff's I had not heard before. And, here, I paraphrase, "People are always saying, how can we help others? What can we do for them? We can give them what they need...if a man is hungry, you give him food." I know that my impulse to give a poor man a cigarette is not a great act, but acting from my own understanding is *something*. Within a few days, Lord Pentland asks me to work for him in his office in Rockefeller Plaza.

Even before I leave California for New York, Lord Pentland asks me to study shorthand. I am not at all surprised, because I'd had a dream the year before in which he asked me to move to New York to type for him. He also, in that dream, gave me a blank book. I am beginning to think I have some sort of destiny, or appointment, with him. I study shorthand for three weeks and tell him that I have learned it. He seems pleasantly surprised. I do not return to California and he asks me to come and work for him at Rockefeller Plaza part-time.

In the office, three months later, he says to me: "So, Jane, you have been here for some time now. What have you got to say for yourself?" I immediately understand that I need to come up with something quickly, deliver an impression, in order to retain my place. Fortunately, I'd had a moment of self-observation the day before that reverberated deeply in my being. I was also, at the time, working concurrently and part-time for a judge who had become irritated with me for something I had done. I had felt his anger as a knife going through me. It was an extremely painful and visceral sensation. I returned to my desk and put a question to myself: "What just happened?" And the answer came back in a voice quite different than my own: "It is because you have no self-respect." I tell Lord Pentland my experience. He affirms that this is true and this causes me additional pain. But I know now that he can help me. He tells me that I can continue working for him. Shortly thereafter, Julie Hanidis, his secretary of many years, quits, and he hires me full time. She tells him that now that I have shown up, she can leave. He tells me that I am the first secretary he has ever hired from within the Gurdjieff Foundation.

One day we were at the British Embassy in Washington, D.C., where I had helped him put together a seminar on British cast iron and steel for the international subway business community. This was one of the two British businesses he represented in New York City. He had asked me to make name badges for all the participants. Then, standing in a circle among ten businessmen at the end of the conference, he looks at me and says in front of everyone (all of whom, except for one, were not compatriots in the Gurdjieff Work), "Where is your name badge?" I have to say, with inner shame, "I didn't make one." And he replies, "You see who you forget to remember. You forget to remember yourself."

I had not, of course, forgotten to make a name tag for myself, rather I had intentionally not done so, thinking I was not important enough to warrant identification. Of whatever healthy sense of self a person might have reasonably developed in youth, due to the loving attention even unenlightened parents might give a child during their upbringing, I had precious little. My sense of self had been shredded, due to reasons better left for later. But what I did have, from the age of four, was an awareness of God (more about "God" later) central or intrinsic to a vast universe. This accelerated into a search at the age of 17 when I became convinced there was a teaching in the world that could help me to understand and experience more of myself and of life than I was presently seeing and experiencing.

And so, in the manner of the miraculous that operates in all our lives, I found the Gurdjieff Work. Coming home late one evening I headed for the kitchen table, where I found – directly in front of me – P. D. Ouspensky's *In Search of the Miraculous*. I sat down and read it throughout the night and into the morning, knowing that I would go anywhere in the world to find people associated with it. Later that day, I asked my brother and sister-in-law whether they had put the book there. Neither he nor she had ever seen the book before nor had they been visited by anyone the night before.

One day he asked me, while we were going up the escalator at Bloomingdale's to buy lighting for his apartment on 66th Street, "What is conscious labor and intentional suffering?" I thought for a while (about fifteen seconds) and said, "Going to work for you every day?" I was not trying to be funny. Working every day with him was not exactly a walk in the park. He replied, "Almost, but not quite." Over the years, I have given this question much thought, as Gurdjieff indicates that practicing conscious labor and intentional suffering is a great hope for us. It is critical to understand this, and I have verified that the ability to suffer myself, and enter into the sorrow or internal conflict rather than run away from it, leads to the possibility of contact with the Higher centers in me. And that sorrow and joy are ultimately proportionate to one another, even if the joy is to come after we shed this mortal incorporeity.

He said to me about working together in the office, "Anything could happen to any of us at any time." At the time, I took this to mean that the doors of perception could open unexpectedly. And often they did. His *being* forced me to be present to myself, and it was not a pretty picture. I had, as both of us knew, very little self-respect. I'd had a variety of traumatic experiences in childhood, and for this reason it was hard for me to receive his loving attention. But I loved him, and he knew this. One day, he had an unexpected visit from Lise Étievant late in the day. While he was in his office with her, I was seized with an impulse to wish for his being and pray, that is, *wish* for his being, and I did so. They were still in his office when I left for home. The next morning, early, Lord Pentland phoned me. "Thank you," he said, "Thank you for everything." I knew that he had felt my wish.

I am at the Workhouse in upstate New York. Madame de Salzmann (Gurdjieff's first disciple and head of the teaching worldwide after his death) is talking about the silence. I do not understand, having been in the Work only a short time, and I think the silence she speaks of must be for the older pupils. It is coffee break and I am sitting on the grass. All at once, I am plunged into silence... and then a wave of the cacophony of the normal mind... and then the deep silence. I realize that the Work is precisely for me – it is not for an elite or priestly class. And there are no intermediaries. I am beginning to develop self-respect. I am beginning to remember myself.

Again, we have spent the day upstate at the Workhouse. My efforts to be present result in my body being filled to the brim with energy. It is years before I can formulate that the methods we practice bring to consciousness that which is dormant and suppressed. It brings what is dim into the light of day. I am sitting on the edge of my bed, experiencing agitation. Suddenly I cannot breathe. I think I am going to die. I imagine how sad everyone will be that I have died so young. Won't Lord Pentland be sad that he worked me so hard? I imagine my funeral and who will be there. Then – all at once – I *know* I will be present at my own funeral. Death is a change of form, but it is not the end. I know this with everything that is in me.

At work the next day, I tell Lord Pentland of my discovery. "Quite right," he says. "Now that you know life is just a question of doing time, how will you live your life?" After a pause, he continues. "For myself I decided living my life in the Work was the best use of my time." He then said, "I bet you think I wanted this Work." When I answered yes, he surprised me with his response. "No. I went to one meeting, and then I wasn't going back. Ouspensky sent people to get me." He said to them, "Go get Pentland."

He then asked me if I understood why I saw what I did, about death being an illusion. I said, "No. I don't." He replied, "It's because you took your thought to the end." I understood immediately then that to censor impressions impedes the natural development of thought, no matter how undeveloped the thought may appear to be. That is why we are told to watch *without changing anything,* to observe ourselves simply, without analysis, at least in the beginning. I realized that if I had obeyed conventional thought, for example, believing that I shouldn't have self-pity, I would not have seen what I did. Since then I have understood that I might follow a thought to its conclusion. In that way, I extend the impression and give birth to it, and that to cut it off in judgment is to abort its life and my own understanding.

Lord Pentland asks me to come to his apartment on 66th Street and read to him a lengthy Sufi text about the seven kingdoms of Heaven. It stated, among other things, that if you look at the sun through your eyelashes at a certain time of day, you can see the kingdoms. After the reading, he says I can ask him any one question. "Is it really true we live other lifetimes?" I ask. "I mean to say," he replies very strongly, "we live thousands and thousands of lifetimes."

I am sitting (meditating) at the Foundation. I am sitting directly to the left of Lord Pentland. I am working hard. Suddenly, my heart burns with heat, and I am immersed in a very bright light. My eyes, though closed, can take in everything in the room. Instantly, I see that Lord Pentland is two. One is sitting in his suit next to me, the other is walking around the room. At the end of the sitting, we proceed out and I ask if I might have a word with him. "It was very hot in there," I say. "Oh," he says, "Do we need to adjust the temperature?" I say, "I'm not talking about that." He pauses, looks at me, and says, "First there is heat, then light."

We are sitting in the library at the New York Foundation. He has steered me to read Mircea Eliade and the study of symbolism. I am so young, I do not yet understand that there are collective symbols in the human psyche that spring up in art and religion throughout time and across cultures. He is talking to me about symbols, and then he says, apropos of nothing, "Study the institutionalization of the Work."

It is only years later, after his death, that I understand what he means by the institutionalization of the Work. And I know now that Gurdjieff left his Work for all his grandchildren, and that serious work can and will take place outside of the institutions, by bringing the Work into life, not just for our personal salvation, but for the good of all.

# PART ONE

———————

## THE OFFICE

# THE LOST PAGES AND SUSTAINED EFFORT

Lord Pentland has just come back to the office from the funeral of Mme. Olga de Hartmann. He realizes that he has left his briefcase, with the notebook of all of the exercises given to him by Gurdjieff, in the taxi. He is naturally concerned and hopes that someone will return it but, as the days pass and it does not arrive, he asks me to start calling all the cab companies in New York City, not a small task. This I do, diligently, day after day.

After several months and calls to every cab company in the city, it occurs to me to abandon the task, as it has obviously not yielded results. I go into his office to suggest that I stop. He somehow intuits what I am about to say, "Don't even..." he says sternly.

I continue calling. Months later, I get a phone call from the accountant for the Gurdjieff Foundation. The briefcase has been returned to him, as his name was on one of the papers. Lord Pentland's briefcase had been tossed and left in the trunk of a cab for many months.

As noted in the Preface, more than a decade later and suddenly, about three years after his death, all that Lord Pentland said to me untethered in my mind, and came rolling forth as if on a reel. I started to faithfully record these memories on paper in a file I carried with me at all times. The memories came daily. I wrote many pages. This unreeling went on for three months and stopped as abruptly as it began.

A year later, I am living in Sonoma County, California, and commuting to San Francisco to work. I get in my car at the end of the day and notice that it has been broken into and my tote stolen. It does not occur to me until I get home that the Pentland file and my precious notes are gone. It is too late to drive back to the city and what would I do in the dark anyway, at night? In a panic I call a coworker who lives near the office about the missing pages. She says she will go out and search the neighborhood in the morning. The next day, she goes out and finds that the thief has strewn the pages about on a very steep street on Portrero Hill. They are everywhere. But she recovers every single page, not one missing.

The similarity astounds me. These stories must be told.

---

We are at a meditation at the workhouse in San Francisco. It is a lengthy sitting. Lord Pentland has given an esoteric exercise about separating our awareness from the physical body, and having the subtle, etheric body move about. Fascinating material, but I am utterly exhausted and hoping the sitting will end soon. Suddenly, Lord Pentland wails and pleads with us: "Don't give up. Keep going. Go another minute. Don't stop." It is as if something great is at stake here. I can still hear his voice pleading with us.

The lesson I derive is this: Don't *ever* give up the effort. Every minute of work has merit.

I am reminded of Gurdjieff saying to his pupils "no effort is ever wasted."

## AT THE OFFICE

In addition to his work as President of the Gurdjieff Foundation of New York, Lord Pentland worked regularly at two British businesses he represented in the United States. One of those business involved conducting geological surveys throughout the world for U.S. mining and oil companies; the other involved representing a British steel foundry that manufactured materials for subway tunnels around the world. An electrical engineer by education, he was very well organized and disciplined in everything he did. I said to him one day, "You know, people are surprised to hear that you actually run a business; they think all you do is the Work." He acknowledged that people did mistakenly assume this.

He came to the office daily, when he was not traveling, and worked at these businesses, as well as Gurdjieff-related business, consulted with people in the Work, and worked on the publications. He tried as well to keep Dick Brower – who worked there also – and me from killing one another. He called the file cabinets that separated Dick from me the "walls of Jericho." Of course, in later years I came to love him.

In the afternoons, I made Lord Pentland Turkish coffee on a hot plate, served with a couple of cookies. Then he would go into his office and close the door, emerge an hour later, and head over to the Gurdjieff Foundation for the evening's activities.

With regard to sleep (a dull, unawakened state of mind, one that we might spend most of our lives in) he told me this: "When you sleep, sleep well." I assumed he wanted me to understand that if I am going to sleep, which is inevitable, that I do so without guilt or shame, that I not undertake activities that lead to self-recrimination – awfully good advice.

I have never met a person less identified with food than Lord Pentland. He ate the same thing for lunch the entire first year I worked for him. Unfailingly, every day, he requested a tuna fish sandwich. After a year or so, I asked him: "Do you think you might like to try something different?" "Like what?" he asked. "Well, you could add bacon to it. And you could have it on toasted whole wheat bread," I suggested. "All right," he said, allowing me to get him that. Thereafter, for the next couple of years, he asked for tuna fish with bacon on whole wheat toast.

He developed pneumonia one winter, and I could hear his lungs whistle while he was in his office. He came out and asked for a cigarette – in those days we smoked like chimneys (and ate bacon). I hesitated. "I have a conscience, you know," I said to him. "Give me one," he said, and so I did.

In the office I strove mightily to remember myself as much of the time as I could, to rouse myself from a habitual state of identification or fusion with my thoughts, and to sense myself wholly in my body – in other words, to practice the Work I had found or which, as it turns out, found me.

One day, as I walked into the Ladies Room across the hall, I encountered my *Self*. It was a luminous presence, as bright and broad as a sun. It was *nothing* like the melancholic personality I often inhabited. I began to understand that I am not what I think myself to be.

On my way to work in a taxi one morning, I looked up to see New York as a gleaming, celestial city. I *saw* that the city I live in is but a blunt reflection of the luminosity it actually is. At the

6

time I saw that, I had not read *Pilgrim's Progress* or knew of Plato's cave allegory. These experiences demonstrated to me that what lies behind or beneath appearances can be apprehended spontaneously.

Lord Pentland had a safe in the office where he obviously kept valuable materials. One day as he was looking through it and I was sitting nearby, he *promised* me, in an impassioned tone, that I would someday hear Gurdjieff's voice. He had such a tape of Gurdjieff speaking in that safe. He said that the voice would not be as I might expect. I know that today one can hear Gurdjieff's voice on You Tube, but I am sure he was telling me that I would someday actually hear Gurdjieff's voice.

I am in the office, wondering how to know what we sometimes call God, a controversial name at best for the loving, ineffable, warm, conscious and numinous particle inherent in all things. A telex comes in from our parent company in England. "*God* morning," it says. Not proof of course, but synchronicity at its most delightful.

Shortly after I started working for him, Lord Pentland makes a comment to Dick Brower, my coworker, about my surname, Gold, referencing its value. I tell him that my mother's maiden name was Diamond. He calls me "this precious jewel." I was then not one of those people that had a healthy ego. I had very many negative feelings, stemming from physical and emotional aggression in my childhood. One day he says to me, "You need love, support and encouragement." I don't think that I had ever put that together in my mind.

## AWARENESS AND SENSATION

Lord Pentland sits me down in his office, early in my tenure there, and asks if I have ever been given sitting instruction. I tell him no. He walks me through the practice of sensing one's limbs, circulating one's attention, and adding a count to occupy the mind of associative thinking. This is one possible first step in meditation practice, to more consciously inhabit the body. I am filled with light and energy from this initial effort. He says, "That was my work. Now make it your own."

I have come to understand that imbuing our bodies with our attention can heal much of what ails us – for example, it remediates anxiety almost immediately. It also almost immediately reduces the fusion with associative thinking, the source of so much of our difficulty. Depositing our attention in our body functions as an anchor for awareness and self-observation. It helps emotionally and physically. It is an entryway to the Kingdom of Heaven within.

Practiced over time, many wonderful things can develop from this practice, including the descent of the Higher in us. Stillness, coupled with the anchoring of the attention in the body, can invite the appearance of more subtle perceptions.

Lord Pentland tells me to sit every day. It is okay to miss once in a while but, on the whole, one should sit every day. He also says, "You can have an impression every day." I come to see these impressions as *mana*, our daily bread.

Madame de Salzmann comes to the San Francisco Foundation. I remember that she tells us we need to sit three times a day. That unless we do, the world will *tomber*, fall down.

When I contemplate the hell world we live in today, I often think that sitting in silence is the act that can save the world, if it is not too late.

Occasionally, during the workday, Lord Pentland would remind me: "Lower down, Jane, lower down." There are many wonderful things inside of us – centers of perception among them – but our center of gravity is lower down. It is not, is never, the mind of cognitive thinking. The mind itself can never bring peace, but a sensation of the whole of myself has that possibility. In Japanese, the word *hara* means belly, or soft belly. It is also understood as that place in the body where the elixir of life is created. It is definitely not in the head.

There is much to say about this practice, so simple and efficacious at the same time. But to be understood it must be practiced.

# CENTERS

**M**me. Jeanne de Salzmann, the person Gurdjieff left in charge of disseminating his teaching after his death, lived in Paris but visited New York annually. She was in New York and Lord Pentland invited me to see her latest Movements film being shown in a small screening room with Madame and others. The Movements are exercises and dances (some with a long and esoteric history) designed to communicate objective truths and produce alternate states of consciousness in the participant. There are many other ways to speak about them. They are a precious and extraordinary part of the teaching.

When we are leaving in the elevator, he asks me why the Movements in the film are in the order that they are. I have no idea. "Higher intellectual center," he says.

---

Lord Pentland shows me the cover of an issue of *Material for Thought* (a review of books and articles published by the San Francisco Gurdjieff Foundation). On it is a photograph of a Native American man holding his head with his hands, a furrowed brow and eyes scrunched shut. "What is he doing?" he asks me. I cannot say. "He's thinking," Lord Pentland responds, reminding me that real thinking is an actual effort, a deliberation, unlike the thoughts that our brains automatically produce and which can cause us no small distress. I learn from self-observation and he validates that the intellectual center is actually quite slow. This is not to be confused with the formatory apparatus, that part of the mind that associates quickly in words – this is not actually thinking.

---

In the office I am standing at the copy machine making copies. I enjoy the repetitive rhythm of putting the paper into the machine and having the copy come out. Lord Pentland watches me and says, "Moving Center, just like me." (I don't think so.)

---

I am standing alone in the hallway after dinner during a work period when Lord Pentland approaches me and says, "You can either be open or closed. You cannot be both at the same time." Long years have shown me that it is far better to remain open, even with its attendant pain. It is a far better option than shutting down, which I have also tried.

Before he invites me to go to New York, there is an evening of Gurdjieff's *extraordinary* – there is no other word for it – music. I am sitting as far back as I can from the piano, knowing what happens when I hear that music. As soon as the music begins, so do the tears. Although I am not making a discernible fuss, about twenty minutes in he comes and gets me, and takes me back to his room to talk. He tells me that my reaction is the "degradation of a finer emotion," is nonetheless consoling, and we talk of many other things. I am puzzled as to why he cared enough to do that. And I am not so sure he is right in his assessment. It seems to me that tears are no degradation at all. As William Blake said, "...a tear is an intellectual thing." And, as Gurdjieff said, "Can learn many things through feeling only."

———————

A friend of mine wants to speak with Lord Pentland and knocks on his door at the Workhouse. Lord Pentland opens the door, and tears are streaming down his face.

We are in the office Wednesday morning, after the Tuesday evening talk at the New York Foundation. Lord Pentland asks if I'd been there the night before. "Yes," I say, "and you were brilliant." He smiles broadly, very proud of himself. "Really?" he says, "What did I say?" But I can't remember. It was a general sense of his particular brand of genius. "I don't remember," I say. "That's all right," he says, "I can never remember what Mme. de Salzmann says to me either."

The words are not the thing.

When I read transcripts of what Lord Pentland said in meetings, I am always struck that the words fail to communicate the vitality of the exchange. There was an energy, a current, inherent in the exchange. Something was transmitted, but it was often not – for me – in the words. The words have importance, but they are far from the thing itself.

I ask him if, when he is speaking at the large, general meetings, he experiences what he is talking about. "*Sometimes,*" he says. I always felt that he was direct and honest, at least with me.

———————

I say to him one day, "Lord Pentland, people act as if you were a God." "It's awful, isn't it?" he says.

———————

We are in the subway and he says, "All you need is one good

friend, to whom you can say anything." He tells me he has such a friend in England and I am happy for him.

# HARD TASKS, EXTRAORDINARY OUTCOMES

On several occasions, Lord Pentland asks me to do things that run counter to my personality that, at the time, was that of a basically good and relatively honest young woman, if somewhat cautious and superstitious.

He asks me to go to the passport office in lower Manhattan to get him a visa for East Germany. He intends to visit the Emile Jaques-Dalcroze building in the suburbs of Dresden. As Mme. de Salzmann had been a Dalcroze student of dancing, he wanted to see the specially outfitted building. He tells me that, in no uncertain terms, he does not want to have to go to the passport office himself.

Clearly, I have to concoct a story to make this happen and I am very anxious about having to lie. I understand that lying to a federal agency can put me in jail, but I have a task in front of me, and I cannot get arrested. I tell the agency that I work for a gentleman, an English lord, who is quadriplegic and whose sole desire in life is to see this building in East Germany, but he cannot possibly make the journey downtown given his severely impaired state.

Gian Carlo Menotti, the great Italian-American composer, is there being sworn in for some reason I cannot ascertain. Lord Pentland is sitting in his air-conditioned office at Rockefeller Center, and I am sweating it out in this dreary government office. I completely understood why he did not want to go there.

The visa is granted. I had accomplished something that I had thought impossible.

In those days, one could not get into a bank after 3:00 p.m. One might be able to get through on the phone, but you could not deposit or withdraw money. On a particular day, Lord Pentland asks me to get a check deposited after 3:00 p.m. He doesn't care how or what I have to do, but I must make it happen. I call the bank and plead with a vice president, and the bank unlocks its doors on Fifth Avenue for me to bring the check in.

Lord Pentland has shown me that I can do more than I think I can.

But a most extraordinary outcome of an adventure is this: One day, Lord Pentland says, "Let's go to the McGraw Hill cafeteria and have lunch." As we are walking there, he tells me that we have to sneak in, because only employees are allowed. So here I am with this ectomorph, impossible to miss by any standard, slinking along the walls in spy mode so as to avoid detection. I am mortified, but follow suit, and of course we get in without ado.

After lunch, we go to the McGraw Hill bookstore. On display are multiple editions of the hardcover magazine, *Horizon*, an erudite publication on history and culture. He stops in front of the display. I happen to mention that it was my father's favorite magazine. He points to one of six different editions, a Gainsborough painting of an English couple on the cover, and asks me if I want a copy. "No, thank you," I say. He repeats: "Do you want this?" "No, thank you," I reply again.

Then he yells at me, very loudly, in the bookstore: "DO YOU WANT IT?" "Yes, thank you," I say, realizing that, for some reason only he knows, he wants me to have it. I then accept it, and take it home with me to read to find out what the necessity was of my having it.

First, on the front cover is that Gainsborough painting of the aforesaid English couple, to the manor born. The man in the painting closely resembles an Englishman with whom I'd had a personal relationship and his wife in the painting resembles me in the present day. Furthermore, the couple's surname is the same name as my father's given name. When I see this, I feel that even if he did not sanction that relationship, Lord Pentland is at least acknowledging that there was something genuine about it. The man and I had thought we'd had a past life connection, and I wondered if it was as that couple.

Seeing this, I feel that something has been resolved about that matter, and proceed to read the rest of the magazine, when, lo and behold, I am stunned to come across a picture of my father in this magazine published in 1976. My father died in 1965, but I recognized the picture because it had been on the cover of *Ad Age* magazine; he had brought it home to show us at the time. My father, because he is the director, is at the center of some fifty people, the number of people it takes to make a ten-second TV commercial. No one is identified by name, but that is my father. I get shivers. The synchronicity is stunning.

I bring the book into work the next day. "Lord Pentland, remember the book you insisted you buy me yesterday?" "Yes," he says. "Well, there is a picture of my father in it," I say. "No," he says, in a facetious tone. "Show me," he says. "That's not your father," he says when I point to him. "Oh, yes, it is," I say. "Your father didn't wear glasses," he says. "Oh, yes he did," I say, "and I know that picture." I tell him its story. He seems pleased and so am

I. It is not the first time Lord Pentland has returned something of my father to me.

Now that I am older and have some kindred experience, I know what goes into perceiving at the level, for example, of the *Horizon* incident. I should say that it is related to hearing at a different level or octave. There is a knowing that comes not in language, but from another place.

In my mother's house, I find an old handblown bottle with a handwritten label marked, in script, *Calvados*. My father had traveled extensively and brought back many interesting things, among them, this bottle. As Gurdjieff spoke so lovingly of Calvados, it seemed fitting to offer it to Lord Pentland. I gave it to him one day saying, "This is from my father to you."

The following year, he asks my best friend to prepare dinner for my birthday at his apartment on 66th Street. He invited some of the people we were closest to for a celebration and, at dessert, he trotted out the bottle of Calvados, which touched me deeply. The Calvados was like fire and I, along with the others, proceeded to feel the effects of it.

He asks me to say something. "I can barely remember myself," I say, "so it means something to me that others remember me." I am touched by his genuine kindness and affection. I did not have enough of that in my upbringing and he knew that without my ever having to tell him.

———————

He tells me in a taxicab one day, "Your father died too soon." I cannot reply. I can barely speak of my father without weeping. I ponder it for many years. And I come to the same conclusion: my father died too soon.

I am sure that Lord Pentland elected to act toward me as a good father might, watching over me, teaching me, and leading me back, again and again, to my own self.

———————

A year and a half after my father died when I was seventeen, I dream I am walking in beautiful rolling hills, as I imagine the Elysian fields of Greek mythology to be. Far off in the distance, there is a large and stately oak tree. As I draw close to it, I see there is a man standing beside it and, as I come up to it, I see that it is my father. "Daddy," I say, embracing him gingerly over an invisible line that I sense, fearful that I will hurt him due to his illness. "There is no suffering here," he tells me. I decide I want to go there where there is no suffering. I begin to step over the invisible boundary, but he stops me. "You can't come here yet," he says.

# THE BOOKS

During the time I worked for Lord Pentland, he published *All and Everything, Beelzebub's Tales to His Grandson* in paperback; *The Third Series, Life Is Real Only Then When 'I Am'*; and *Views From the Real World*.

In preparation for the three-volume *Beelzebub's Tales* in paperback, Lord Pentland had another student and I proofread the entire book, word for word, a task for which I will be forever grateful. This forged, as well, a friendship of considerable respect for the man I worked with and imprinted in my mind the book itself.

The Third Series, *Life Is Real Only Then, When 'I Am'*, was prepared from the originally typed manuscripts. After a long day of work at the office and evening meetings, I would then go home to type the manuscript late into the evening. After it was typed and prepared for publication, Lord Pentland had me read the entire book to him before sending it off to the publisher.

When I finished reading the book aloud – it took several days – Lord Pentland said, "Next time, take a breath at the commas and periods." I was mortified at my lack of awareness of my own physiology, i.e., the way I breathed. I wonder still why he did not tell me this as I was reading. Maybe so that I would have an impression of my own idiocy, rushing through something like that. I understand now that it was related to my chief feature.

I find The Third Series to be an extraordinary document in which Gurdjieff shows himself to be utterly human and emotional. Of interest, he indicts Americans for their psychotic "self-remembering" and prophesizes that Gurdjieff clubs will proliferate in the Third Millennium. And here we are.

*Views From the Real World* was also typed from the original manuscripts of the meetings in a similar way, working all day at the office, going to meetings, then hopping a train home to type late into the evening. He was teaching me to work beyond my capacity.

The book needed a title. Lord Pentland came out to my desk one day and said, "I think we should call it, *'Man is a Plural Being.'*" He seemed rather pleased with himself. "Not good," I offered, as I did not think it covered the material sufficiently, but his point was not lost on me. I studied the multiplicity of I's in myself for years thereafter. It is surely one of the chief features of our psychology.

If you've ever wondered, the encrypted aphorism on the cover of *Views From the Real World* says: "Remember yourself, always and everywhere." We solved the script during a work period at St. Elmo.

I see now that these tasks related to the publishing, so laborious at the time, were gifts from Lord Pentland, and they implanted Gurdjieff's thoughts and ideas firmly into my brain.

———————

For a project, a calendar was to be made of Gurdjieff's aphorisms. Lord Pentland asked me to choose twelve, one for each month. This I did, but he did not accept the one I chose for August. He could see that I had a peculiar morbidity associated with that month, and rejected the one I chose, opting instead for one that affirmed life. I continue the struggle to antidote a morose tendency with an affirming thought. More recently, my mind has begun to do this automatically, demonstrating that new habits can be formed even later into life.

# HUMOR

**L**ord Pentland calls from San Francisco one day and asks me, "Can you guess who is here with me now?" I cannot, so I ask him who it is. He tells me that Don Juan, Carlos Castaneda's Toltec teacher, is there. This was not so far-fetched as one might think, since we knew that Castaneda and some of his pupils had been to the San Francisco Foundation. I had heard stories from a friend who spent time with them, astonishing stories, straight out of Castaneda's books – one about a bird turning into a human being along the side of the road right in front of my friend's eyes. One day, two of Castaneda's pupils came down to the weaving shed at the San Francisco Foundation. To me they looked like deer, innocent and otherworldly.

Then he asks me, "Would you like to ask Don Juan a question?" I didn't want to miss the opportunity, so I had to think fast. And I did come up with one. "Okay, put him on," I say, "I've got a question."

"April Fool!" he says, laughing uproariously at his own joke.

I understood from him that to have a question is more meaningful than to have an answer. It feels to me to be a higher state of mind. But this feeling goes against our conditioning that calls out for knowing and certainty.

———

Someone says to him, "Lord Pentland, it seems to me that you are one step from Buddha." "Yes," he replies, "and it's a mighty big step."

A friend has just moved to a new apartment. Lord Pentland asks him for his new phone number. My friend says, "It is so new, I don't remember it." Lord Pentland says, "Well, then give it to me approximately!"

———

I tell Lord Pentland that a man in the Work wants to marry me. He is not, however, a suitable suitor. Lord Pentland says, "My dear girl, your mother would have a heart attack."

———

Approaching the Work does not have to be dour. It can be light and joyful, just as life occasionally/rarely/often is.

A friend of mine who worked on the publishing team says that Lord Pentland was involved with the design of the front cover of *Transitional Man,* a book very worth reading. The cover is simple and graceful with shades of blue from light to dark on the cover. My friend tells me that, during its design, Lord Pentland said, "They want seven, let's give them seven." And so, there are seven shades of blue.

On a day when Lord Pentland was out of town, an energetic, rumpled older man came into the office. "I need to speak with Lord Pentland," he said urgently. "Who are you? I asked. "Fritz Peters," he said. "I've always wanted to meet you!" I exclaimed, excited and feeling very fortunate to meet the man whose book, *Boyhood with Gurdjieff*, has profoundly touched so many of us. I was also frankly grateful that Lord Pentland was out of town, so that a friendship might be forged.

I took a good look at him and said, "You stay here. I'll be right back." It looked to me like he needed rations and, in those days that would have been coffee, cigarettes and a donut, which I promptly purchased and gave to him. It was the beginning of a real friendship.

As it happened, Fritz badly needed cash and had come to sell a manuscript of the *Third Series* to Lord Pentland. Lord Pentland eventually gave him some money for it, not that he needed the manuscript. This was more about helping a man who had fallen on hard times.

Fritz had massive energy and was happy to weave his tales, including the horrendous, tragic stories of World War II and the stories of Gurdjieff so beautifully wrought in *Boyhood with Gurdjieff*. He was especially proud of his book, *The World Next Door*, and the fact that e. e. cummings had told him that the first sentence of that book was the best first sentence in the history of the English language. "The shadows are the first to go" is the first sentence in his description of the mental illness that was to dog him episodically throughout his life.

Fritz was a complicated man. He'd had a difficult childhood, passed around to various adults. He told me that one of his parents was mentally ill. He was raised by female intelligentsia and artists in Europe; this is how he came to know Gurdjieff and stay at the Prieuré. And he was a gay man in a time when it was largely considered a moral transgression to be so. Add to those a mental illness that in retrospect looks like schizoaffective or bipolar disorder (I say this as a mental health professional) *and* post-traumatic stress from the war, and you have genuine chaos. Fritz spelled trouble everywhere he went, but I knew him to be kind and extremely witty. As Gurdjieff said, "Where there is much good, there is much bad." That was Fritz.

Fritz had a problem with alcohol that Gurdjieff spoke to in one of his books, suggesting that there were times Fritz could drink and times he could not. We certainly drank quite a bit together. I understand in hindsight that it was Fritz' attempt to medicate the symptoms of the savagely difficult mental disorder that he suffered from.

In his later years, Fritz worked as a legal secretary in New York and lived in an old residential hotel. I was able to arrange a meeting for him with Annie Lou Staveley, an old friend of his from the Prieuré. He subsequently spent some time at Annie Lou's Farm in Oregon, where I do believe he stirred up a storm. He later moved to Albuquerque, where I visited him. It was Lord Pentland who later called to tell me that he had died. I am glad we were friends, and that I could extend a hand, and he back toward me.

He especially tried to help me with the negative effects of my chief feature. He implored me to count to ten before I said or did *anything*.

Fritz had a heart attack before I met him and I first heard about the near-death experience from him. He told me his consciousness left his body down below and his awareness hovered above him, watching what was happening as the doctors in the hospital cared for him.

––––––––––

Fritz introduced me to the mystical work of John Donne and to the sermon that Donne delivered Easter 1619, on the occasion of the King being mortally ill. This sermon Fritz would recite over and again with tremendous passion:

> We are all conceived in close Prison; in our Mothers wombs, we are close Prisoners all; when we are borne, we are borne but to the liberty of the house; Prisoners still, though within larger walls; and then all our life is but a going out to the place of Execution, to death. Now was there ever any man seen to sleep in the Cart, between New-gate, and Tyborne? Between the Prison, and the place of Execution, does any man sleep? And we sleep all the way; from the womb to the grave we are never thoroughly awake; but pass on with such dreames. And imaginations as these, I may

live as well, as another, and why should I dye, rather than another? But awake, and tell me, says this Text, *Quis homo? who is that other that thou talkest of? What man is he that liveth and shall not see death?*

# PART TWO

———————

## DOWN FROM ABOVE

# THE MIRACULOUS

It is Summer, 1981, in San Francisco. We are in a week of intense inner and outer work, consisting of meditation, practical arts (cooking and sewing), fine arts and crafts (woodcraft, weaving, pottery and bookbinding), writing and translation, and sacred dance (that we call Movements). Lord Pentland calls me into his room and hands me a box. "This box is especially for you," he says. It is a tin of Walker shortbread with a picture on the front of Prince Charles and Lady Diana, commemorating their engagement. He opens it up, apologizes for the lack of shortbread, and shows me that there is nothing in it.

I gave much thought as to what the meaning of the box might be, because Lord Pentland was not a man given to meaningless gestures. I knew he gave it to me for *something*. On the face of it, I thought the picture of an engagement suggested I have hope that one day I might find my other half, one marriage having already failed.

Further, more elevated, thought gave rise to the idea that the meaning of the box was in its royal couple and that I ought to be looking toward the conjunction, or alchemical marriage, the sacred *coniuncto,* that is talked about in alchemy – the marriage of the male and female inside us, or the union of the soul with the Divine, within me.

But mostly I kept the box close to me, and used it to remember my teacher and his gifts. It thus became an object of contemplation.

Lord Pentland left his body on February 14, 1984.

Presciently, years earlier, in a telephone call from him in California to me in New York, he asked how the weather was. "Very cold," I said. "Wait until the second week of February. That is the coldest week of the year," he responded.

By 1986, I was having a very difficult time. I was in severe emotional distress issuing from unresolved past trauma. Although I was meditating regularly, and experiencing the grace and warmth and love that it can be, my life was very hard. I was alone with two small children, without family or community support. And although I worked for a living and had some refuge in my studies, late one night I found myself in acute grief, sobbing, in a grave and dark night of the soul. That night, when I could find no respite, I did firmly petition God to show me a sign – something, *anything,* of the Immanent Presence.

Two hours later I was still awake, now frozen in grief, when a very tall, slender specter appeared in my bedroom, to the right of my bed, and appeared to hop over, as it were, to the place where the box was. And then, at 3:00 a.m., without a move on my part, there was a loud rap on the Walker Shortbread tin.

It did not end my pain, but I had asked for a sign for the first and only time in my life and had received one. I knew then exactly why Lord Pentland had given me that empty tin. He knew that someday I would need that kind of help, and that I would be open to receive it.

The meaning I derived from it was that there was a purpose to this veil of tears, and that I was not alone. Then and there, and on this Easter that I write this many years later, I know with all my heart and soul that the Resurrection of Christ is real, available, however rare, and not mere metaphor. I am not saying this is that, but it bears a resemblance.

The following morning, at 7:30 a.m., in a stunning display of synchronicity, I received a call from Mary Sinclair, Lord Pentland's daughter. She asked if I was willing to write something about her father for the Gurdjieff Foundation archives; that she and Lady Pentland, who was to arrive there shortly, wanted to put something together for the Foundation archives.

I shortly discovered the wisdom of the dictum, "Neither cast ye your pearls before swine." One of Lord Pentland's elder pupils, with whom I shared this good, nay great, news denied it and walked out of the room when I told him. I do believe he even said, "Bah." But it was a miracle, which Gurdjieff defines as the appearance in one world of the laws of another. Gurdjieff gave his teaching for all, and such truths and perceptions can and do appear to people, not just an elite or priestly caste.

It was not the first time I had experienced Lord Pentland's presence not-quite-in-the-flesh, but it was the first time after he had passed. Nothing was heard from the Walker shortbread tin again until 1990 when, upon returning from a vacation in Yosemite, I walked into my bedroom and found that the box had fallen, face down, on my dresser. I knew that something had happened. A telephone call moments later confirmed that something had indeed happened. Dick Brower, the only other person who worked in Lord Pentland's office with us, had died unexpectedly.

---

John Pentland was a work of human art. He crafted himself to a high degree of being. He served many, many people. He was also flawed. But human flaw does not deny us our possibility. It is the crucible in which we toil.

In a conversation once, long before, I said to him that I was waiting for a miracle. And he said, "That's fine. Just do something while you're waiting." And I do: I try to act with intent, awareness, serve something, assist people, as he asked me to. There have been other miracles, and these are also told herein. But every day, every perception – that we are here at all – everything in creation is itself a miracle, and sometimes it is so hard to see that this is what this is.

## "IF YOU WORK CONSCIOUSLY, CONSCIOUS SPIRITS WILL BE SENT TO GUIDE YOU"

I t is Yom Kippur 1988, just two years after the etheric visitation from Lord Pentland, and four years after his death. I am not a religious person by any means, but from time to time revisit the religion of my birth. I remember that Gurdjieff said that one of the ends of his work is to return a man or woman to the religion of their birth.

The Yom Kippur service has ended. We leave the synagogue. I turn to my friend – a Gurdjieff cohort – and say, "I'm not sure I believe in God anymore."

A brief detour about the word "God." When I use the word "God," I am talking about an omni-conscious, astrophysics-quantum physics God; a warm and loving emanation; not a man-on-a-cloud God, or an incarnation God (though it could be), or a God of dogma. I am talking about a unified field theory God, a particle or spark of light in you and me God; an Immanent and Radiant God. And I believe that God is love and is present in every single thing.

My doubt came from having a rough go of it, raising the two children on my own, struggling with the negative traces and conditioning of my bloodline. I had not yet understood that everything that comes, it comes from Above, including sorrow. Nonetheless, I sat in meditation every morning for forty-five minutes, putting myself in the hands of the Higher, promising to tell my story if my life should change. I had to give it over to something Higher, because I could see that my own efforts were not going to bear much fruit. I didn't really understand what I had to do to improve my circumstances. I wished only to be of service, to have a service vocation. "Please let me serve" was my prayer.

I sat this way in silent prayer asking for help for one and a half years.

Coming home from temple that Yom Kippur evening my telephone rings. It is my brother. He tells me that his fiancée, Whoopi Goldberg, has decided that she wants to support my children and me for four years so that I can go back to school. On Yom Kippur, when for the Jewish people their fate is sealed for the next year, I am delivered this astonishingly beneficent news. And I promptly registered to return to university after an absence of eighteen years.

How it is that a Jewish girl had not received a college education is another story.

I feel and think many things about the good fortune that befell me. I know, as Gurdjieff says, "If you work consciously, conscious spirits will be sent to guide you." I feel that trying with sincerity to come under the influence of the Higher is a wiser petition than asking for *anything*.

I do not know if Whoopi coming in and out of my brother's life was of any lasting benefit to him. He acted badly toward her, in spite of her enormous generosity to him and his family. But out of her largesse toward me came two degrees, and I was able to put into action one of the final tasks Lord Pentland gave to me, "You should help people," he said. "You probably already do."

The Christmas of my first year working for him, Lord Pentland gave me the book, *Psychology and Religion*, by the Jungian

James Hillman. He must have known I was a born therapist. Fifteen years later, when I registered to return to San Francisco State, I put down Psychology and Religion as my major and minor, respectively, remembering that his gift coincided with my true interests.

I have found a place in life. In my professional work, much of what I implement I learned from Lord Pentland and Gurdjieff. I consider my work to be atonement for transgressions against myself and others. And I cannot help but wonder if it was Lord Pentland who brought about this great good fortune, two years after his passing, carving out a path for me that I am grateful for every day of my life. But it was Whoopi who gave me this gift, and I remain deeply obliged to her. It is said of Whoopi that she is one upon whom rests the dust of the ages. This is very true of her; she has a timeless, eternal sense about her.

## WHAT WILL CHANGE THE WORLD?

After work, Lord Pentland and I are having a drink in Charley O's, the restaurant downstairs from his office at 10 Rockefeller Center, before heading over to the Foundation for the evening's meetings. "What will change the world?" he asks me. I whine, "I don't know, I have a narrow mind." "No," he says, "You have a broad mind. What will change the world?" he asks again.

"Conscience?" I venture. "No," he says, *"Emanations will change the world."* He wants me to understand the effect that emanations have, that my emanations have. It is a different way of seeing the world, seeing it in terms of energies and vibration, rather than seeing change in terms of morality or duality; rather than actions, to understand it in terms of the unseen. Needless to say, these are related, but it is about working from a different place, a place of emanations.

At moments, I can check my emanations. I can know for myself that what I emanate is a help to the world, or not. I can, as Lord Pentland said on many occasions, *"Take your own measure."* If I say I care about the world, I will check my emanations.

Years later, in San Francisco, Lord Pentland reads a paper he wrote in which he lists the ten most important ideas of Gurdjieff. I recall that his primary idea was conscience. Obviously, an act of conscience will emanate differently than an unconscious act.

––––––––

Lord Pentland returns earlier than expected to New York and calls me at the office to let me know he is back. He asks me emphatically to *tell no one* that he is back in town. Before long, I get a phone call from someone with whom I admittedly have a competitive relationship. This person wants to know whether Lord Pentland would be back in town Friday, as he had been told. Operating from pure ego, I say that he is back already.

I am wracked with guilt. I cannot get it off my back, no matter how hard I try. It dogs me on the train home. I endeavor to justify my behavior to myself and I cannot. I get off the train and walk home. I pick up some ironing. I realize there is no way out. I can only accept what I did. And at that moment, there is an opening: I am in the starry world, the heavens surround me.

I will transgress, being human. But if I can accept the full weight of my actions, there may be hope for me.

Gurdjieff says of human beings that they "justify, justify, justify." There is no egregious behavior I cannot try to find a way to worm out of. I remember that Christopher Fremantle, another of the elders at the New York Gurdjieff Foundation once said, "Even when we know we're wrong, we think we're right."

I knew enough about how Lord Pentland worked by this time to know that he had set me up so that I could have an impression. That was one of the ways he taught: setting you up, not saying explicitly what he was doing. Helping you to have an impression, helping you to work. He once told me "You can have an impression every day." Each day I can see myself. I can hold a wish for myself and others. I can understand something.

I n response to a letter I sent him, Lord Pentland wrote "Life is not pleasant." It shocks and annoys me. For although I had experienced a certain amount of unpleasantness from childhood on, I hadn't fully accepted it would always be so. Immersed in the culture, I believed I should be happy and that it was a failure on my part that I was not. As well, I had a melancholic turn, perhaps acceptable in Europe, less so in an America that urges us to be cheerful and keep consuming in spite of massive suffering on every side.

I wonder what Gurdjieff would have to say about the conditions of modern life, calling them as he did then, abnormal. If they were abnormal then, what would he call them now, abominable? A combined scourge of materialism, greed and egotism profoundly obscures any divine template, a blueprint from Above (having nothing to do with organized religious dogma) that could help us to organize life on earth with compassion toward all who live here.

In *Beelzebub's Tales*, Gurdjieff tells us that there is hope for man, if he would only realize that "everyone on whom his eyes rest is going to die." I took that task seriously and practiced it for a year and a half with no discernible results. Then one day at the San Francisco Foundation I looked at a woman with whom I had virtually no relationship, and who I believe had an antipathy, or something, toward me, and in one moment realized fully, without a shadow of a doubt, that this person is *going to die.* It was a shock to learn that she nearly lost her life a week later. We do not entirely comprehend the effects our efforts may have.

I was interested in death from a very early age, perhaps due to a major surgery at the age of 4, when I had the first glimpse of a vast universe. This interest led to my becoming a Hospice volunteer, sitting with people who were in the process of dying, so that I could see death up close and try to close the gap between my fear and the growing sense and knowledge that we go elsewhere when the coating that is the body gives us up. The great soul Nisargadatta puts it thus:

> Once you know that death happens to the body and not to you, you just watch your body falling off, like a discarded garment. The real you is timeless and beyond birth and death.

And in response to a question put to an unnamed Master about whether death was real or illusion, the Master replied: "Death is a real illusion."

Even science is getting on board with this – that consciousness extends beyond the body – as a respected scientist recently speculated that when the body dies, the consciousness moves to another universe. In Gurdjieff's system of thought, we could say that it goes to another world, as the worlds interpenetrate one another. My own unscientific theory is that the elusive dark matter in the universe is actually indicative of the force of the other worlds or dimensions that interpenetrate one another, but are not visible to the naked eye or with the technology we have at present. As the Christ says in the Gospels,

"In my father's house, there are many mansions."

Be all that as it may, the passage from birth to death is a journey that entails – for most on this planet – at least a degree of suffering. It could be physical, mental or emotional, but on every continent, everywhere, there is suffering. On this, the Buddhists are preeminent.

What does Gurdjieff tell us about this suffering? He says that we must "consciously labor and intentionally suffer." I would not presume to understand completely what he means, but what I have come to for myself is that I need to take it on. That instead of trying to make the suffering go away, or bypass it through an ill-conceived notion of spirituality, I need to enter into it. In that same letter of Lord Pentland's noted above, he writes: "Stay with the conflict longer." Not run away from, not strive to be happy, stay with.

That *staying* may well result in more, rather than less, sorrow. As Gurdjieff exquisitely puts it: "We can lighten as much as possible the Sorrow of our Common Father." Indeed, as we begin to awaken, our compassion for others, and ourselves, begins to grow.

Further, Gurdjieff tells us "for every sorrow there is a corresponding joy." And I put my faith in that, for experience shows that when I am able to suffer more consciously, my capacity to feel joy and love increases.

## HIGHER OCTAVES OF COMMUNICATION

I am at the Gurdjieff Foundation in New York, working part-time with the secretary there, and part-time for Lord Pentland in his office before he has hired me full time. William Segal (a cohort of Lord Pentland), Lady Pentland, the Foundation secretary Lois Bry, and I are sitting in a circle, talking about some administrative matter concerning Gurdjieff's music. Suddenly, there is a shift in consciousness. Bill Segal and I are turned, as if by an external force, to face one another. Something in our chests is having a dialogue. It is not in words, but something is communicated. It is a conversation about love, Real Love, what we are all looking for, to feel and to be. I think later that this must be the language of the heart.

At that time, Bill Segal was not someone with whom I'd had *any* relationship. We'd never even talked. A few weeks after that experience, he was in a horrendous car accident that laid him up seriously for many, many months. He never looked the same again. I wished for him with all my heart during his recovery. He has a long recovery and comes to the Foundation again. When he sees me he says something. It is the first time actual words have been spoken between us.

———

I am living in Mount Vernon, New York, sharing a flat with my good friend, Dianne Edwards. It was Lord Pentland's idea that we room together and support each other through the vagaries of working for him in separate capacities, she at the Foundation, me at his office in Rockefeller Plaza. We are getting ready to take the train into Manhattan to our jobs, when we hear in the vestibule the voice of our downstairs neighbor. The shock was that we knew she was visiting her relatives hundreds of miles away. We look at each other in astonishment. We do not even mention it until we are on the train.

Yet another time, she and I are reading Tarot cards. She looks at me and suddenly bursts into tears. She tells me later that a force flung her to the floor. When she calms down, I ask her, "What is it?" She says that I had turned wholly into moving purple and yellow molecules. When she asks Lord Pentland about it the next day, he tells her, "Don't identify."

There are higher octaves of communication, just as there are higher octaves of perception. We can see with our eyes closed. We can hear what is happening hundreds of miles away. We can see energies, what our true makeup is. We can speak with our hearts. Thoughts are real things and are molecular, material.

When we are spending the day at a friend's house, I ask Lord Pentland, "What is the most unusual experience you have ever had?" He ponders for a moment and chooses this one. "Time travel," he says. "I had to pick Mme. de Salzmann up at the airport, and I was running late, by half an hour." She was coming in from France and he was in a dither about being late. "The next thing I knew, half an hour had elapsed and I was at JFK, on time."

This same day, I ask him, "Is God merciful or severe?" He says, "God is both merciful and severe." I think to myself, just like you.

Later that day, he tells a story how at Mendham someone had asked him to shovel manure and that he declined to do it. This runs contrary to what we are told in the Work about obedience to tasks. Later in the day, he asks me to take out the garbage. I do not take out the garbage. Not after that story, I don't.

He tells me one day at the office that, when he was at Mendham, he would stealthily remove and copy Ouspensky's papers. I know that he is telling me it is fine for me to copy and take whatever I wish.

"We are both more and less than we think we are." Lord Pentland

— I —

I am sitting in a Mexican Restaurant in the Mission district of San Francisco. It is chaotic at our table, with many friends and a big family with five children. The waiter is surly and unpleasant. His negativity disturbs me. He asks me what I want, and I ask for a substitution. He is not having it. I have been working with the power of having a question, so I put the question to myself: "Why am I here?"

Suddenly I am propelled into the starry worlds, the heavens surround me. Something, somebody, is communicating with me: "What is the origin of life?" it says. The words reverberate in me and echo in the starry world.

At the same time, I am in the restaurant with these people. No one has noticed anything. But my consciousness is deeply altered. For the next few days, I feel as if I am in a sea of consciousness, and my ego is partly shattered, broken up.

The next day, I break out in a rash all over my body, a crazy itchy rash. It lasts for weeks and even at the University of California Medical Center they cannot diagnose it. I realize that the body, at least my body, may not be prepared to withstand higher experiences of this nature without preparation. The process of meditating can be likened to tuning an instrument. We want to know the Higher right away, but it takes time for us to form a relationship with it, for trust to develop between us. And time perhaps for the body to acclimate to the finer, higher energies that descend from Above.

I tell Lord Pentland of my experience in the restaurant. He reflects, "Sometimes our questions are very deep."

— II —

It is an extended work period at the San Francisco Foundation. We sit in silence several times a day. In the sitting this particular morning, an energy comes from Above, and appears to descend in me through the top of the head. It is a quiet, deep and sober joy, and it is intelligent. It permeates my body. It wipes the ego clean. It informs me of everything I need to know. There is nothing else to be desired.

At the end of the sitting, it is difficult for me to return to my work as kitchen head. I have undergone a deep shift. I understand that were we to be often in this state where the Higher descends in us, it might be difficult to operate in the world. How do I live in the world with the ego wiped out? It takes me a couple of hours to return to a normal ego state.

In the state where a finer energy descends, the ego assumes a smaller, more rightful place. It is as if in a smaller compartment. It is not an idea; it feels to be an actual location.

— III —

Again, I am in a sitting at the Foundation with the group and for the second time in my life I am able to see with eyes closed. I can see 360 degrees around me. And I see that there are Beings of Light. One of them approaches me from behind and adjusts my spine so that it is fully erect. With that adjustment, the energy flows yet more vigorously from Above.

I mention to one of the elders about the beings of light and she chafes. "There are no beings of light," she tells me. I find Paul Reynard (our Movements teacher) and say, "There are beings of light in the movements hall." He says, "It's all right."

— IV —

Home from the work period, I continue to experience this descendent energy whilst sitting in silence. I am sitting one morning before the day's activities begin, and I hear activity in the kitchen. My son, who is six years old, is cooking something up. At the moment the energy is poised to enter my head from Above, I hear him approaching my bedroom. I sense that he is carrying precisely the same energy as the energy hovering above me. This holiness, this sacred energy, and his bringing me a fried egg, are one and the same. It is all holy. And then, in my own idiocy, I raise my voice to him for interrupting my "meditation."

Two years before, we were at a flea market and my then four-year old son asks for fifty cents to buy me something at an adjacent booth. He brings back a small china figurine of a boy holding a fried egg. What does this concordance mean, this gift of his and two years later a fried egg coinciding with a penetrating, loving energy, and a remorse that will linger?

I am "shit mother," as Gurdjieff would say.

— V —

I am going to a theme discussion at the SF Foundation. I am new there, so I don't know all the rules about who sits where. I go to the front row, and someone tells me I cannot sit there. My feelings are hurt. Suddenly, I am plunged into a light so bright that it obscures everything. I hear that someone is speaking, but it is as if it is taking place in another dimension.

The next days, I find living in the world very difficult, and everything is suffused with light. I am in this luminosity that infuses the world.

There was a time when I would wake in the night, sobbing, hearing myself say, "I want to go home." But there was no home here to go to. My family house was no home. It is some other home I am longing for. I wonder if it is somewhere in that luminescence.

— VI —

Sitting regularly tunes the instrument that is the body. It also informs the Higher that I am available for service, in that conducting this Higher energy serves an evolutionary purpose. As noted earlier, Mme. de Salzmann came to the San Francisco groups and exhorted us to sit three times a day, lest the world *"tomber,"* or fall down.

There was a time when, sitting regularly, I was awakened at five a.m. every morning by something I could not see. It would, as it were, tap me on the shoulder. Called into service, I responded for a long time. And then I didn't.

I forget to remember myself.

— VII —

When I was that small child recovering from that operation, so small that my vocabulary must have been very limited, how did I know that the world was but a speck of dust on the fingernail of God? I told this to a friend one day, and she said that she had just heard someone speak about that exact imagery on the radio (NPR) the day before. I can only think that there is objective information available somewhere, perhaps it is what Gurdjieff refers to as the Korkaptilnian thought tapes that encircle the earth. There is obviously something very deep in us that is not related to our age or ability to speak. When I am with small children, I try to remember and respect this depth within them.

# GOD AND MAMMON

I am sitting close to the head table during a work period in upstate New York, and I see Christopher Fremantle turn to Lord Pentland and say, "Look at Jane." I have no idea what they are looking at. I know that I am feeling pretty good, elated even, from the collective energy and the day's work. After dinner, I am standing alone in the hallway. Lord Pentland walks over to me, smiles broadly, then turns it off, and says: "Ye cannot serve God and Mammon."

I do not know what Mammon means and eventually look it up. Mammon is material greed or wealth, often portrayed as a deity, the God of wealth. I have never been all that interested in money. But what if Mammon represents the world, with the drive for acquisition, of endless craving for one thing or another, an experience, even something Higher?

Then it is apt advice for me. I am not so dedicated that I seek the Higher all the time. Throughout my life, one thing or another captures my attention. My search is ephemeral, unsteady. I feel like a misfit in this world; I believe and have seen into the unseen and am mocked for it. It interests me passionately and I affirm it. But I am not wholly committed. And woe unto she who is "between two stools."

I understand Gurdjieff's plaint in the Third Series, his wailing that he cannot remember himself. I am never in that much grief about it, which is why I will never get to Gurdjieff's level, as Lord Pentland tells me one day at the office, apropos of nothing in particular. "You might as well face that you are not going to get to Gurdjieff's level in this lifetime," he says. I tell a friend that he has told me this. She remarks, "How compassionate of him."

———————

I am standing at the copy machine in the office. "What are you seeing?" Lord Pentland asks me. I tell him frankly, "I see that I don't care about the Work." He validates this. "That is *exactly* what you have to see," he says. To be honest, I am longing for a husband and family. Not that I am especially prepared for it, or will be able to do it well. Sitting in his office together one afternoon, he says to me, again apropos of nothing: "Even if you find the man of your dreams, you'll still have a search." He also tells me then, "You don't always marry the love of your life."

It is my birthday and he takes me to lunch at the Spaghetti Factory. He calls over the resident palm reader. I am sure he knows that she is astute at what she does. He says I can ask her one question. And I am sure he knows what the question will be.

"When will I meet the man of my dreams?" I ask. She looks at my palm and says, "It will be a *long* time before that happens." Lord Pentland tells me, as we are walking back to the office, "She is right, it *will* be a long time." I am pulverized by the news, but eventually accept that, given my injuries, it will take me a long time to learn how to love and be loved. What does long time mean, I wonder. Never? I don't want anything less than the real thing anyway. But I don't know how I will bear the loneliness.

That Christmas, he gives me an original edition of A. R. Orage's book, *On Love*. So, apparently, I am to study love.

There was published in 1981 by Far West Editions a wonderful small book called *Transitional Man*, by Franklin Earnest III. It was rumored back then that Lord Pentland in fact wrote Chapter VI, essentially a treatise on love in the broadest possible sense. He acknowledges that he collaborated on it in the Introduction to the book. Love certainly seems to me to be consistent with the aim of the Work.

> If the brain seizes upon just one idea such as the wish "to love," it is equipped sufficiently to carry that idea eventually to its fruition, but to handle such a charge, its circuitry must be made ready to receive and process it.

———

A woman married to a man not so very bright asks Gurdjieff: "How do you love someone who is stupid?" Gurdjieff responds: "That's what love is."

———

In a few years I meet a man I can love, and have a family with. When I first meet him, there is recognition. A thought passes through my mind. It says, "I have known him for three thousand years." I have never had a thought like that. Three thousand years?

I am pregnant and Lord Pentland tells me I must marry this man. So marry we do. I am surprised that I feel the presence of something higher at our marriage on the beach at dawn in Bodega Bay. I had taken marriage lightly, thinking of the proverbial piece of paper. But there is an unmistakable Presence in the upper left part of the blue sky. Later, when I am doing a sacred movement, a prayer, we are asked to point exactly there with the left index finger.

———————

As my son is being conceived, I look up and there is a Tibetan patriarch in robes, with others behind him, slightly elevated, in the clouds, a *thangka* come alive. It is truly extraordinary what I am seeing. There is a world within this world. Furthermore, there is an exchange of energies of the heart between my husband and me. There is much more to conception, evidently, than we generally have any idea.

We have two children. Difficulties arise. Lord Pentland encourages me to accept my life as it is, and look at it again in six months. After all, he is the father of my children and I should not be too quick to leave.

I eventually decide to divorce. I am filled with fear and remorse. I call Lord Pentland the day before the divorce is final and say, "I don't want to do the wrong thing. I want to do the right thing." "Yes," he says, "that is because you remember something from long, long, long, long ago," elongating l-o-o-o-o-n-g. There it is again: there is a long history with us.

My former husband died last year, having become a dear friend, one of the best. I was present at his passing, when his being left his body. As he is dying he says, "I am trying to find a new life." I feel that our journey together is complete.

The Dalai Lama has said the quickest path to enlightenment is marriage. That may be easy for him to say as he is notably not married. Marriage is a human, social construct, even though it may have its roots in a divine archetype. That doesn't make it any easier.

———————

I bring my three-month-old son to meet Lord Pentland in San Francisco where I have been living. He tells a friend of mine in New York, "Jane's son has Universal Love." As he grows, I see that it is true – he is remarkably free of judgment, and is drawn to animals, trees and children. Living in this world is very hard for him. But he manifests universal love to a remarkable degree.

I meet a Tibetan lama and ask him what it was I saw that night, the night of my son's conception. He tells me that when a child is being conceived, sometimes the child is shown who his parents will be, is introduced, as it were, to them.

Later in life, my son is not doing so well. He elected to go into the Navy and saw combat. He is injured by explosives. Awful things happened and his life is quite challenging. But I remember that he comes from another world, I saw into that world. He remains remarkably impartial about people, never gossips, and is deeply loving and accepting. He does indeed have universal love, just as Lord Pentland told my friend.

When my daughter was born, and I was living in Santa Cruz, a Gurdjieff friend came to help out. When she returned to San Francisco, Lord Pentland asked her, "What is the baby like?" Our essence must be that obvious, right from our births, if you know how to see it. My daughter is a mathematician, and though she has had numinous experiences herself, she does not like to speak of them, for they are very personal and outside scientific knowledge.

My children have taught me how to love and be loved, each in their own, very different way.

---

I have recently noticed with the death of friends that I am left with a strong sense of their essence in the days after their passing. The personality that may have been the source of difficulty for them or for others is as if vanished, replaced by their core, the beauty of their selves. It is so joyous and bright.

---

During preparations for a Gurdjieff birthday celebration, Lord Pentland tells the man who is heading up the decorations in the Movements Hall that, if he wants to know what is beautiful, he "should talk to Jane Gold." The man tells me this as we are flying to Los Angeles for a Movements film. I am confounded as I had never thought of myself as having especially aesthetic sensibilities (although he did ask me to help him decorate his apartment on 66th Street). It is only years later that I understand. He wanted me to love myself, to have the right kind of self-Love. This I could not then do.

---

It is 1999. Sitting in my living room one evening, something comes to me and says something like, "I am a boy spirit and I want to be born." The same thing repeated the following night. Too important to ignore, I phoned my son and told him that, even though I am aware that he and his wife are not trying to have a child, there is a male spirit hovering around wanting to be born. I do not think he took me seriously at all. Nonetheless, four months later, he tells me that his wife is pregnant. I say to him, "It is that boy that wanted to be born." And, indeed, Gabriel was born the following year. Kinship with grandchildren is a mystical affair – Gurdjieff didn't entitle the book *Beelzebub's Tales to His Grandson* for no reason – and my relationship with this child is profoundly close to this day.

We have come from another place and have divine origins. As Teilhard de Chardin, the French priest/philosopher, says,

> You are not a human being in search of a spiritual experience. You are a spiritual being immersed in a human experience.

And,

> Love is the affinity which links and draws together the elements of the world... Love, in fact, is the agent of universal synthesis.

———

I have a date to meet a dear cousin, a person I am very close to. I am at the appointed building in the small foyer at the appointed time. People come and go but he is not one of them. I finally go out into the street, and he drives slowly past me. I am running in the street, trying to get his attention, but I cannot get to him. I have the distinct feeling that there are entities playing with me, and not in a good way. It has a sinister, malevolent feel. I speak to my cousin later that evening. He had indeed seen me there, a woman wearing the clothing I had on, but did not recognize her as me. I cried that forces seemed to prevent me from this meeting.

The next day at work I tell Lord Pentland of my experience. "What do you do when you see that your life is not in your own hands?" He responds, "You live without self-pity."

———————

A friend is sitting with his Sufi teacher when the teacher says, "See that homeless man across the street? I have to go and talk to him. No one knows this, but he runs the city."

We cannot judge the life of another person. As Gurdjieff says, "Judge no one. Man 50% good. Trust no one. Man 50% bad." I have come to believe that judging someone harshly is an egregious offense. I feel there is no longer a place for it in my Work. Discernment is one thing, judgment another. You cannot determine a person's interior by their external manifestations, or their personality. As a Sufi saying goes, "Your Lord knows best who is rightly guided."

———————

A true teacher will show you how to figure things out for yourself. They won't interpret or correct your experience. Lord Pentland never denied me my experience or interests. On the contrary, for example, he sent me to the Second World Conference on Kirlian Photography and the Human Aura, at a time when these types of things were beginning to be taken seriously and scientific method applied to them. He also around the same time sent me to workshop on Journaling – this may well have been the germination of the 45 journals I now have that chronicle this life that is dappled with the numinous among the mundane.

---

I participated in a Tibetan ceremony, an initiation into Life and Death. I figured if I was fearful of death, I had to be afraid of life also. I am looking at the Lama who has come from India to help us. I am looking at him, and there is an enormous gleaming diamond in thin air a few inches above his head. Years later, at a friend's wedding, I meet a lama who is a student of the lama with the diamond. I tell him about the diamond. "What does it mean?" I ask him. "I don't know," he says. "You don't know?" I query him. "No, but how nice for you," he says. Note the absence of ridicule or the knee jerk reaction that it is imagination. He reaches over to the very large Buddha and pulls out a photograph of the lama with the diamond, Sakya Trezin, his teacher, and gives it to me.

## RAY OF CREATION

There is an idea in the Gurdjieff cosmology called the Ray of Creation. It seeks to explain the order of creation and existence in the Universe according to cosmic laws, laws which have a numerical equivalent. I have always assumed that the experiences recounted herein where I was in the starry world were on another rung than that of Earth on the Ray of Creation.

According to this idea of the Ray of Creation, the Earth (or its equivalent elsewhere) is very far from the Center of Creation. In fact, we are next to the last stop, so to speak, which is the Moon, where the "weeping and gnashing of teeth" takes place. Even a cursory view of this world we live in will demonstrate that we aren't that far away from the weeping and gnashing of teeth. There is no use complaining about how awful it is here. Only our own efforts will help us to evolve the earth beyond its current state.

It is a January 13th celebration of Gurdjieff's birthday at the New York Foundation. There is a strong current of energy and I am trying hard to remember myself, to embody a prayer and a wish for all of us. Just then, I see where we are on what Gurdjieff calls the Ray of Creation. We are far from the Center, but we are not forgotten. It is a shock to see the vast scale of things.

———

There is an old Hassidic story. The old Hassid keeps two notes, one in either pocket. One note says, "I am nothing but dust and ashes." The other, "The Universe was made for me."

I began the Gurdjieff Work in New York in 1968 under the aegis of Christopher Fremantle. After reading *In Search of the Miraculous*, I sought out the Work and a psychologist I had been friends with helped me to do so. The following year I moved to San Francisco. When I got to there, Lord Pentland, whom I'd not yet met, called me on the phone, and said, "Christopher said I should keep my eye on you." We first met shortly thereafter in a group. At this first meeting, I could see that he had deep insight into things and people, and he seemed to know what I was thinking. I was very intrigued by him and felt free to express myself. I took efforts thereafter to make sure that he noticed me, because I wanted to partake of who and what he was and what he knew. We met again privately to talk about things; at that meeting he told me that he liked me. I liked that he was direct and honest.

----

It is one of those times when I have taken a leave. A friend of mine from New York sees Lord Pentland at a gathering and she says to him, "What happened to Jane? She is my friend and I miss her." Lord Pentland responded, "How do you think I feel? She was my friend too." When she tells me this, I feel remorse and weep. I had hurt him, I knew that, by the way I left. No matter how brilliant or how extraordinary a being he was, he was very human and had real feelings. But I must atone for the hurt I have caused, and not only toward him. I think it must be humanly impossible to love people and not hurt or be hurt by them. Seen in this way, remorse has transformative properties. Woe unto him who has no remorse.

One such foray away from the institution of the Work was when I had moved back to San Francisco from New York and found work in a criminal law practice. The attorney I worked for told me that there was going to be a party and rug sale at the office later that evening. In the afternoon, a group of people arrived and proceeded to put up carpets and decorate the office. Later that evening, people arrive – I know them. They are my fellows from the Gurdjieff Foundation. I am glad to see them and I return.

There is another time that I have taken a leave. This time I am working at another law firm, a corporate firm, and I discover that the attorney I have been hired to work for is in fact the attorney for the Gurdjieff Foundation. I return yet again.

The Work has found me thus three times. I never left the larger search, and I always remained a student of the Gurdjieff ideas. I feel it is important to remember that the Work is vaster than any one expression of it. And it has always been clear to me, as Gurdjieff said, that "life is the Great Teacher," not an institution. And there was never an injunction from Gurdjieff that one remain in the groups forever.

I recently heard some elder complain about me being absent from the groups for a time. If there is an ignorant question, it is this, "How long have you been in the Work?" It's a small-minded question. It's the wrong thing to be counting. It is the whole of a person's life that counts, not the time one spent belonging to a particular institution or church. Lord Pentland expressed this brilliantly, and with humor, this way:

A woman at a work gathering, a beginner obviously, someone who didn't know Lord Pentland, asked him, "And how long have you been in the Work?" He looked at his watch and said to her, "Oh, about an hour."

———————

When I return to school at San Francisco State in 1988, I take a class in Consciousness. The teacher is showing the class a film. It turns out to be a video of the Art of Living lecture series put on by the San Francisco Gurdjieff Foundation. As it begins, Lord Pentland comes onto the screen and looks with complete presence into the camera. Once again, I am stunned. He is not with us in-the-flesh anymore, but I clearly cannot escape him, not that I was aiming to. He is my teacher in this life. We are linked.

# MORE LESSONS

We are in Northern California, and Lord Pentland is taking us for a drive. As we return to the house where he is staying, his behavior turns oddly morose and melodramatic. "Oh," he wails, "Christopher (Fremantle) is dying. His body is falling apart. It is terrible. It is awful. He is in so much pain." He is really laying the misery on hard.

By this time, I figured that he is trying to communicate something. Often he uses the didactic method. He wants his pupils to find their question. The question, I am learning, is more important than the answer. So I formulate my question:

"Well, how is he spiritually?" I ask. Lord Pentland brightens, and his mood, that had clearly been an act, changes. "Spiritually," he says, "Christopher is wonderful. Spiritually, he is very bright."

I was afraid of dying at one point in my life, so I decided to become a hospice volunteer. I thought I should get very close to death, to look at it up close. One of the first things I noticed is that there is luminosity, a warm and loving emanation surrounds the dying person. In some cases, it is clear they are seeing things and beings we do not see. The dying report visits from those who have gone before, sometimes long before. A woman I knew, just before she died, told me that she was "looking forward to the adventure." And a simply spoken rancher, as he was dying, is reported to have said, "Gosh, the inner, the outer." My own father, as he dies, says, "Ah, death!"

Another friend, not given to these types of experiences, says that, as her grandfather is passing, she looks into his eyes and sees the whole universe in them.

I verify again and again that the life of the body is separate from the life of the spirit. I am learning from the hospice work that there is help at the end. "We are never alone, never forgotten," Lord Pentland tells my friend, quoting the Gospel of St. John.

The first thing I notice when I approach the dying patient is the luminosity and warmth surrounding her. Her face is blue and sallow, she is frail, dying, but everything else surrounding her is bright.

Some who are dying speak in metaphors of travelling as, for example, "Where is my passport?" and "I am on a raft helping others to cross to the other side."

Earlier this year, my neighbor, a frail elder who had been a rocket scientist, is quite anxiously facing death. I want to help him be less anxious, so I ask him, "Have you ever had any unusual experiences in your life, something very out of the ordinary?" He tells me that he has never spoken of this before, but when he was suffering post-traumatic stress after World War II, a man appeared by the side of his bed, tapping a walking stick. My neighbor asked the man, "Are you Jesus?" and the man said, "Yes," and he was then calmed. He seemed comforted by his memory of this visitation from his God.

I remember being in a car with others on the way to a workday up north, driving in the snow and ice, when the vehicle skids and goes into a terrifying spin. It looks like we are headed over a ravine when it comes to a sudden stop, just at the point where we would have gone over. The car is filled with light and radiance.

It cannot be that angels are simply a figment of human imagination. I will never accept the explanation for anything numinous that it is a conjuring of the mind. I was put on a team by Lord Pentland to study John the Scot, a ninth century mystic who details the circles of cherubim and seraphim, not unlike what Gurdjieff does in *Beelzebub's Tales*.

I saw an angel (or something) with my own eyes. I was in Natchez, Mississippi with a friend who was adamant about going down to the delta that evening and finding an authentic juke joint to hear some blues. Two California women in miniskirts, red lipstick and dangling earrings showing up at a blues shack in the deep south by the river seemed like a very bad idea to me. But she was insistent and I could not convince her otherwise.

Just then, a man approaches us from the left and starts talking with us. He tells us his name is Ray Cardin, that he is a musician and that he is from Spartanburg, South Carolina. My friend tells him we'd like to hear some blues and are thinking of going to find a blues shack along the delta that evening. He excuses himself and says he'll be right back. He returns holding an album of music, to show us that he knows whereof he speaks. The album has his name on it. He says that we should not go to the Delta but instead head to Beale Street in Nashville, where we will really enjoy ourselves. There will be music, dancing in the streets and good Southern food. I feel enormous relief. He says goodbye and then heads off in the opposite direction from whence he came and, as he is about twenty feet away, he simply disappears into thin air. We are both struck dumb, look at each other, and eventually say, "Did you see that?"

The next day we are exploring the Great Smokies and run into a man who is studying the local flora. He has lots of good information for us about the local biota. He tells us his name is Ed Engel, which means angel in German.

———————

I have learned not to confuse the body, its life and its pain, with that which is spiritualized or eternal in us.

At the beginning of a Movements film, Mme. De Salzmann is quoted, "Nothing lasts forever, nor ends completely."

———————

Lord Pentland asks me to visit him in Marin County. I get there just as he comes to the top of a stairway, sees me, and says: "Everyone has their point of view." I am young and naive, innocent enough to think that there is an objective truth to situations; that there is right and wrong, especially in human relations. I am quite sure there is an objective conscience, a Ten Commandments, another Code of human behavior. But he is telling me something else, and I am frankly annoyed by it. If everyone has their own point of view, how will we ever be able to solve the problems on our planet?

———————

Lord Pentland tells me one day "You don't owe anybody any explanations." This frees me from justifying my actions to others. It is enough to know what I must do, and do it. This is a powerful tool – not owing anyone any explanations, especially for women who often feel they must explain their actions to others.

I have just told Lord Pentland of an extraordinary perception I'd had that resulted in my being, yet again, in the starry world. This shook me to my core. I ask him, "Did that really happen?" "You just told me it did," he replied, thus engendering in me the beginning of trust in my own process, trust in my own perception, my own point of view.

———

I am very pregnant on a drive with Lord Pentland. I am talking about the experience of being pregnant. I am telling him I have read a book about conscious childbirth. It is obvious that this is not his favorite subject. "But what about the body Kesdjan?" he asks me. "Does the book say anything about that?"

# TRUST IN THE PROCESS OF YOUR LIFE

A tragedy has happened in my family. Perhaps I should step in to take care of my newborn nephew, as his mother has had a post-partum break. I don't know whether I should stay in California or move back to New York. I ask Lord Pentland what I should do.

"Let Providence have its say," he says. "Trust in the process of your life."

It is some of the best advice I have ever been given. No, it is the best. It bespeaks a profound grace and intelligence operating in our lives.

It flies, however, in the face of the ubiquity of suffering in our world. There is almost no way to understand the enormity of human suffering. A rational person asks, eventually, how can there be an intelligent or loving Prime Mover who would allow the suffering to exist? And how can I possibly be all right even in myself with all the suffering around me?

I have come to understand that without suffering, I would not have learned what I have. Certainly, I would be less without what I have lived through. I used to wonder about the long-suffering Job, and I could not understand why he was so great, until I realized that everything that comes, it comes from Above, even the adversity, and he understood that. I saw this once: that all the adversity that I cursed in my life was in fact a blessing. It is, however, nearly impossible to see when you are going through it.

I remember Lord Pentland telling me to "Trust in the

process of your life." And I look at the totality of my life, at its beauty, the questions, the great mystery, the sorrow, and its call to love. And in it I now find much meaning.

Without darkness, there is no light. There is no coming into the light, without having been in the dark. Without suffering, what would be our possibility? It seems a remarkable process, a brilliant trajectory.

"For every sorrow, there is a corresponding joy," Gurdjieff says. I can see that now. They are never far, the one from the other.

Without suffering, I would never grow. Without suffering, I would be robotic, hedonistic. It checks me. It has a similar function to certain human emotion. Though difficult to bear, suffering keeps me human, keeps me working.

The suffering all around us presents us with an opportunity. Rather than try to obliterate our suffering, we are called to enter it, to suffer it intentionally. Lord Pentland says to me in a letter, "You must stay longer in the contradictions."

Will I look only to my own salvation? Or will I see that I am, as Krishnamurti said, "the world." I am offered the opportunity here not only to help myself but to help others.

Lord Pentland told us, "When you sit, remember that you sit for all."

"If I am not for myself, who will be for me. *If I am only for myself, what good am I? And if not now, when?*" (Hillel the Elder)

---

When I was struggling to raise two children on my own and deal with the vagaries of my life, I had an exquisite dream, one of those that seemed to be a real experience. In it, I was nearly blinded by light, but I could see a Hindu teacher, and he told me that I must learn that "everything is grounded in the Godhead."

## ON THE WORK BEING CALLED "THE WORK," GOD, AND THE DIFFICULTY OF LANGUAGE

I t strikes me as singularly pretentious to call a system of thought – no matter that it is a profound and comprehensive synthesis of spiritual and psychological ideas – "the Work."

Shocked when a teacher suggested to me that my own mother, over whom I suffered greatly, was "searching for the Work," I apprehended at once that the Work is not confined to any institution or set of ideas but relates to the possibility of human evolution on an individual scale across time and cultures.

And I was equally stopped short when Lord Pentland said to me: "Everyone wants to go to Heaven" one afternoon in his office, apropos of nothing.

Which brings me to the difficulty of discussing the Higher both within and without an institutionalized setting. It is understandable that the word God is difficult for many people to tolerate. Even among the religions, God means something different. For some, it refers to a fantasy, a meaningless fairy tale in a world of injustice and oppression. As I said earlier, my God is immanent and radiant, omni-conscious and loving, in which science and spirituality are not divided, but One and the same.

When I was fourteen and my father was observing the Yom Kippur fast, and I was not, he asked me to respect his fast. I told him that I did not believe in God. He looked at me, lovingly and patiently, and merely said, "You will."

But make no mistake, this God is not outside ourselves. As the Christ said, "The Kingdom of Heaven is within you."

And, as the Sufis say, "God is closer than your jugular." Somewhere in *Beelzebub's Tales* – I read it once but have failed to find it since, Gurdjieff says that each one of us is on a path to God, that it is inevitably so.

## THE BEST KARMA

Simplistic, reductionist thinking leads to speculation that having beauty, brains, wealth, or a good mother or father, is the result of good karma. I find this formulation troubling but prevalent, and American in its narcissism and materiality.

Karma is a word that is bandied about in the culture I inhabit, Northern California, where one's spirituality is as much a credential as one's wealth or educational status. I find these ways of seeing people offensive, and lead to that unfortunate feature of man's psyche, as described by Gurdjieff in *Beelzebub's Tales*, of situating oneself as either above or below another.

So I set upon a search to find a definition of karma I could live with. And I found this: The best karma is having a question about why you are here.

It follows, then, that being born into poverty, or being born blind, for example, while tragic and difficult, are not necessarily impediments toward self-development or evolution. If we are talking about thousands of lifetimes, as Lord Pentland indicated to me, it follows we would experience just about everything in the world. And any condition is fertile soil for my growth and development. What do I need to understand presently, in this life? What particular tasks am I entrusted with?

The conduction or experience of higher energies – a task that is often spoken of by acolytes as the only task worth achieving – is not the only task worth applying oneself to. The universe is so vast, creation so infinite, Gurdjieff's teaching included, to have the same aim for everyone. What if each individual has the task of actualizing himself or herself, and following no lead but one's own inner guidance? "Be yourself, then God and the Devil don't matter," Gurdjieff said.

From time to time, I sought out other teachers, and there seemed to be many more authentic ones on these shores in those days.

It is very, very beautiful here in Switzerland in the Bernese Oberland. My friend and I have come to see and hear Jiddhu Krishnamurti, considered by many to be among the most enlightened beings on earth. As an ethereally handsome teenager, he was anointed by Annie Besant and the Theosophists as the World Teacher. In his twenties he declined that name and position. A virulent opponent of teachers and teachings, he pronounced "truth is a pathless land." I have often pondered that all the wise ones walked their *own* paths, and this is what Krishnamurti is saying, over and over again: Follow your own path.

Krishnamurti gives two to three hours of talks twice a week. The talks are difficult to bear. They are very long and they challenge you to move beyond thought. People come from all over the world to hear him.

He gives no methods. There is nothing to follow. There is no excitement. His voice, emanating from such a small man, is unbelievably powerful. He in no way flatters you. You drink too much, have too much sex, do everything too much, and you don't know how to meditate, he tells us relentlessly. It is exhausting, this challenge. After these talks, I want to go home and sleep. I am not alone in that.

My friend has rented a fourteen-room chalet with

staggering views of the Alps. It is just the two of us, but he is flush from making a fortune.

In this enormous house, there is a bomb shelter in the basement. It is grey metal, with a large wheel to open it. I find it eerie. The Swiss want to survive the unthinkable. A Swiss friend (the "mayor" of such a facility) tells me that they have hollowed out mountains in strategic places so that the population can survive a nuclear holocaust.

Krishnamurti talks about the truth "coming for you," "seeking you out." It has come for him, he tells us. His journal, as I recall, is about that. He says he has profound pain in his brain, as if an operation is taking place deep within in it. He cries out in his sleep. Is this the price one pays for having consciousness come for one? K. has suffered in his life, beaten by teachers when young, the death of his beloved brother. There are rumors that, while he claims to have never had a sexual relationship, in fact he has been carrying on an affair with a married woman. I do not especially judge or begrudge him, though subterfuge is not ideal behavior in a sage. Why do we expect moral perfection? Are we not human? I think if everyone were righteous, we would have no good literature or movies. Why would we even be here?

In the afternoon, following one of these talks, I feel that something is seeking me out. It is not a being exactly, but a force. All day I try to avoid it, pretend it is not there, because it feels like it will overtake me, and I will cease to be, in a way that feels frightening and uncomfortable, and so I naturally try to resist it. But it is *there*, a powerful *presence*, searching me out. I go down to the basement to avoid it, where there is nothing but the laundry, a ping-pong table and the aforesaid bomb shelter, and it catches me. I am then suddenly wholly present, my mind has been erased, there is not one thought. I go upstairs, outside, onto the balcony. It is night and very dark outside. Here are the heavens, in all their glory. There is sound, then silence, alternating. There is no import to anything apart from this *being*. The cars with their lights come and go. The mountains are majestic in their being. It is *being*, beyond myself. It overtakes me, immerses me in Beauty and makes me one with the world. And it goes on.

There is no pain in this. And then I remember, it comes at first as a movement in the brain, and then a specific thought that I want this person I am with to love me, and he well might if I tell him that I have been plunged into consciousness. After all, isn't this why we have come to Switzerland?

And... it is over. I am in a completely different world now. I has reappeared. Ego is back. I try to tell him, and he's really not even interested. But I know now what is possible. It was Krishnamurti's being that brought this about, this erasure and consequent beauty. But I do not understand the mechanism of the transmission.

Later, we go to Brockhurst, Krishnamurti's school in England. Because he was abused as a child by teachers, he is passionate about education and has started schools in England, the U.S., and India, where children can learn in a healthy atmosphere. We drive up to the vast grounds and park. We get out of the car, and Krishnamurti emerges from the house and walks to us. It's a bit surreal, meeting him like this. He introduces himself as K. and shakes our hands. He is the most self-effaced person I have ever met. There is not a trace of ego in him that I can detect, and not much of a personality either that I can discern. He has absolutely nothing to sell, no axe to grind here.

He joins us at our table for dinner. He is so self-effaced, dinner conversation is not scintillating. I believe we talked about food (we'd cooked a vegetarian dinner); K. was of the Brahmin caste. It seemed to me he liked cowboy movies. He was very boy-like in some ways. His personality seemed undeveloped, but his being was one for the ages.

During one of the talks he says, "Don't listen if you don't want your life to change radically." I note that. And, within a week, I am traveling through Europe alone. Life on the outside had been good enough. But Krishnamurti opened something up in me, a part of myself I had shut down, and I began a new round of sorrow, on the inside, for years. Is this sorrow an operation deep inside me, one that will lead to freedom?

# PART THREE

---

## UP FROM BELOW

## THE PSYCHOLOGICAL TEACHING
## OF GEORGE GURDJIEFF

While Gurdjieff left an impressive cosmology, I feel that his psychological teachings have been given short shrift by his students, though he made it abundantly clear that our subjective psychology is important.

That he says "it is a blessing to be born into a bloodline where there are things to be worked out" should be enough to generate inquiry into our own histories. That he gives the task, as explicated by Ouspenky in *In Search of the Miraculous*, to tell our life stories in groups, and to particularly note what we are omitting or lying about, also speaks to the importance of our subjective lives.

Gurdjieff says that the higher centers are always operating in us, and that it is the lower centers that need work, the lower centers constituting our psychology.

Gurdjieff tells us also that the study of human psychology is the study of fear and lying, and that the Real Self disappears in the face of a lie. I undertook to work with that material and would ask myself: What I am I lying about, or deluding myself about today? And I would search myself for the contradictions. I did not then nor do I have now to search deeply for where the fear or lying is, as it is usually not far.

In another reading, Gurdjieff says "The whole of an adult's life should be a struggle between yes and no." Or, one could say, between "I" and "it," "it" being our mechanical behavior. A state of transcendence may be desirable, but struggle with and observation of our own psychology could form much of our daily work.

Recently I was told by some fellows that Gurdjieff says man has no psychology, to which I say, let's not split hairs.

At a large meeting at the end of the workday in San Francisco, Lord Pentland told the group that he had two readings, one about the work of crafts and one about psychology. He asked for a show of hands as to which reading people would like to hear. Everyone, save me and one other, raised their hands for crafts. He went ahead and read the one on psychology. He showed me then and there that the group was not interested in psychology. But in truth, it was not a particularly good reading, and he stopped partway through and switched to the one on crafts. At the time, I was baffled by this, but have come to understand that many people are, indeed, not especially interested in their own psychologies. Tis a pity, I think. Michel de Salzmann, who was a psychiatrist by profession, and therefore intrinsically interested in the human psyche, said in a lecture in San Francisco that the "cause of our conflicts lay in the unconscious." It is worth looking to the unconscious, and there are methods for this.

I have come to the conclusion that human emotion, though an often messy part of our psychology, is an endowment from Above, and that our emotional lives on earth, however difficult or unpleasant, are a gift as well. We are not soulless automatons asked to remember ourselves (and thus go "high") in a mechanical or stultifying way. If anything, we might to strive to live with the same richness, passion and vigor that Gurdjieff demonstrated.

Lord Pentland said to me one day in the office: "You are a human being, not a machine." It confused me at the time because we are told that we are mechanical, subject to automatic behavior about which we can do very little, save for super efforts that stretch us beyond what we imagine we can do. Was he alluding to my penchant for efficiency and productivity? Or was he encouraging me to open to the more vulnerable parts of my humanity? Or that I was not quite as mechanical as I thought I was? He had once shown me a letter his previous secretary wrote to him, saying that now that he had found me, she could finally move on, even if I was, to quote him, "too efficient." I think he might be pleased to know that I am now, without a doubt, much less efficient.

Our emotions can show us the direction of our psychological work. They allow us to take our measure. They are not a mere nuisance and they are essential for our development.

Gurdjieff also tells us to go back as far as our grandfather. He tells us that we can repair the past. Elsewhere, he says that one of the last things we need to work on is our psychosexuality. Yet again, he tells us that in the end our work is to bear the unpleasant manifestations of others. Indeed, just as they must bear ours.

When I was a young student, an elder told me that I was being subjective. As if she or I could through our will or mind alone be anything else. As if it was something other than Grace that renders moments of real objectivity.

Our subjective lives are in fact the path on which our work gets done.

———————

Gurdjieff also tells us that we have within us an 8-year-old, a 48-year-old, and a 108-year-old. That is, the Child, the

Adult, and the Wise Elder. I find this a most helpful construct in my professional work as a therapist. It is a useful touchstone for studying the multiplicity of I's in ourselves as well.

We are encouraged by Gurdjieff to be conscious egotists, that is, not unconscious narcissists. This will only come about through the study of ourselves. We are encouraged to study ourselves for a long time and thoroughly through self-observation before we change anything.

We cannot remember ourselves all day every day. But we can observe ourselves. And, as quantum mechanics demonstrates, the act of observing a thing changes it.

If the Gurdjieff Work today were to admit and explore the depth and perspicacity of the psychological teaching left by him, it would be an invaluable contribution to human psychology and evolution, so sorely needed. For Gurdjieff left both cosmological *and* psychological teaching, each one of deep intelligence and complexity.

We cannot exist only a diet of ideas about the Higher. We are incarnated and have psychologies and histories. We can develop ourselves harmoniously. After all, this was the premise of the Institute at the Prieure. But it is precisely our human self that is the raw material – *the negrido* – for alchemical change – into gold.

## PSYCHOLOGY AND SUBJECTIVITY

Within a year of meeting Lord Pentland in San Francisco, he invited me to come and work for him at his office in New York City, so I relocated from San Francisco back to my hometown. He had told me at our first meeting that he liked me, and the feeling was mutual. I could see that a friendship of a kind was developing, in addition to a teacher-student relationship. And, naturally, I was intrigued by this man who looked and spoke like nobody I had ever met. He seemed wise about not only what I was interested in, that is, the teachings of George Gurdjieff, but seemed to know my psychology as well. I observed how his responses to people seemed subtle and tailor-made, not rote in any way.

My relationship with him as described here demonstrates that, in working with an individual, he worked not only with their possibilities of transforming and conducting energies of a higher level, but with their subjective psyche as well.

It does not always follow that people interested in spirituality are interested in their own psyches. On the contrary, there can be avoidance of subjectivity or, in any case, talking about it. It has seemed to me that folks on a spiritual path often want to bypass their subjectivity, jump over it, go high. The perception seems to be that our subjectivity is beneath us. There is no such mandate anywhere that I can find to support that. To my mind, bypassing our subjective, personal experience and focusing exclusively on self-remembering could, as Gurdjieff clarifies in the Third Series, result in a kind of "psychosis" or depersonalization. To be sure, by avoiding one's personal dilemma or contradictions, one might avoid emotional pain in the short term, but in the long term it is no way for an adult to live their life, unexamined precisely for its subjectivity.

How else, for example, would we ever see what our chief features are, that formation around which our entire psyche revolves? We are told again and again to study ourselves, to observe ourselves, without intervening, to see impartially, objectively, our own subjectivity. And to see it not once, but at least three times, for without repeated observations, nothing will change, nor would we know what to change.

Even the most superficial examination will reveal that we have been conditioned from the earliest age to become what we are. And further observation and efforts will reveal that it is very difficult, if not impossible, to alter some of our most basic character traits.

––––––––––

I was conditioned to think poorly of myself, to loathe myself. I had a malignantly narcissistic mother (I called her the "evil that spawned me"), and a father who, while interesting by virtue of his profession (motion pictures) and interests (multilingual, artistic, aviation, Great Nature) was nonetheless not home most of the time and left me in the hands of this "death mother" and a sadistic brother. As well, I am told by a relative that my mother sought psychiatric help when I was six months old because she wanted to kill me. I had always known that I was a painful thorn in my mother's side and that I was unwanted. Her contempt for me became introjected, that is, I began to feel her feelings toward me as my own. Thus I could not warm to or trust either of my parents and this impacted me profoundly.

Lord Pentland queried me about my relationship to my father who had passed shortly before I found the Gurdjieff Work at 17 and responded in a curious and artful way to my mother, who wanted to meet him.

My mother calls and says she is coming to the office. She would like to meet Lord Pentland. My mother is a woman for whom the superficial things of life are important, and, as such, I am a terrible disappointment to her. Her contempt for my values is obvious, and I never know what mother love is (except I know how to love my own children). Nevertheless, she wants to meet the man with the title. I tell Lord Pentland she is coming and that she will be there at lunchtime. He said nothing then, but emerged from his office in a short while, put his hat and coat on, looked directly at me, and left. I knew his schedule for the day, and knew that he had engagements all afternoon. I also knew, when he left, because of the way he looked at me, that I was not ask him where he was going or when he would be back.

My mother came and went. Throughout the afternoon, people came for their appointments and I had to tell them Lord Pentland had gone out, and I could offer no explanation. It dawned on me, slowly that afternoon, but most assuredly over the ensuing years, that what I needed to do with regard to my own mother was to put my hat and coat on, and go away.

It was clear that Lord Pentland had no interest in meeting that person not because she was any kind of formidable opponent or petty tyrant *for him*, but that I needed to understand that the way to deal with this toxic relationship was to radically detach from it.

I will always be grateful to Lord Pentland for leaving the office that day, and showing me that I can be free. That he inconvenienced himself and others to teach me this, touches me to this day. We never spoke of it.

I once consulted a rabbi about the commandment to Honor thy Father and Mother. I told him that I simply could not honor my mother. He knew her, and he said this: "First you have to have a mother to honor."

Lastly, Lord Pentland asked me why I did not come to his daughter's wedding. I said I was not aware that I was invited. He told me that he called my mother's home, as I was traveling at the time, and had left the invitation with her. She never told me.

---

I found Lord Pentland to be extremely nurturing and encouraging, in contradistinction to how I was raised. No doubt he could see how my conditioning impaired me. He said to me one day, "You are attractive, intelligent and cautious." It was a shock, and I think he threw caution in there because I tended to be quite impulsive.

He asked me, always pointing to the work ahead, "You've gone far. The question is, how far will you go?"

Lord Pentland, in an interview nine months before he died (Telos, The Gurdjieff Journal, Volume 1, Issue 7) spoke of Gurdjieff, "He had an extraordinary quality of providing encouragement." Lord Pentland did the same, though I am aware that with some people he could be quite severe.

When I told Lord Pentland I thought I might have a

problem with alcohol, he said, "Just don't be selfish. Don't drink alone." He may not have addressed the problem with alcohol which I was not ready to give up in any case at that time, but he did respond to the strong tendency to withdraw from others. He encouraged me to go against my conditioning, to stay in relationship with others.

He told me to sit every day. It was okay to miss once in a while, but on the whole, one should sit (meditate) every day. When I told him that I experience a particular kind of energy when I sit, he said, "*I* am the source of that energy." That is, *we* are the source of that energy. It is in us.

He said to me one day when my suffering was acute, "You can't bear yourself." I felt his compassion, to have noted that without judgment.

---

He urged me to get out of bed in the morning at the moment I wake up, not to linger. And to make my bed every day.

---

He told me one day, again apropos of nothing, that I was *pneumatic*. I searched for years for a definition that made sense to me. At last, I came across three definitions in a gigantic dictionary: bosomy, spiritual (of the breath, *pneuma*) and an intermediary between this world and the next. As I was very small at the time he told me, the first did not apply.

---

I had a dream two days before September 11, 2001, that I was high atop two office towers, and they were burning. What does this tell us about the human mind? It tells us that there is a part of us that is connected to the universal and that time is not linear, to see ahead like that. I have no idea why, but I occasionally dream the headlines of a more catastrophic nature a day or two before they happen. I do not know what to do with information like that except pray, or direct my thought, to throw light on a dark situation.

───────────

One day at the office Lord Pentland was being uncharacteristically obnoxious toward me, ordering me around, not giving me enough time to finish tasks, and being unkind. I was troubled by this, and felt bad about myself, until I made the decision to not let it touch me on the inside, to not let myself be affected by how he felt about me. As soon as I shifted in this way, his behavior shifted and he was "himself" again. We didn't have to speak about it, but a lesson was learned about freeing myself from the opinions of others.

## INNER CONSIDERING

L ord Pentland put together a group of a dozen or so people who met on Saturday mornings and did experimental work, mostly consisting of exploring our instincts and centers and their functions. He had another and I lead this group on many occasions; but I had no appetite or ambition then for being in charge or ascending in the Work. I still don't. The group allowed us to observe ourselves in different conditions than occurred at the Foundation. We watched documentaries on subjects that interested us; we met with an avant-garde dramatist and singing teacher; and we studied the Feldenkrais method, among other ventures.

Inner considering is a form of identification with people in which we are overly concerned about how others might feel or act towards us resulting in preoccupation with injustices and resentments.

Lord Pentland told me that I innerly considered less than the other students in the group. I was surprised by this, and then daunted. Because if, in fact, I internally considered less than my peers, we were all in deep trouble.

———————

Lord Pentland told the San Francisco group one New Year's Eve that we could have anything we wanted, but we needed to realize that we were going about it in the wrong way. I recall a similar task given by Gurdjieff, a specific exercise for achieving *anything* (including meeting with those who had passed over to the other side) we wanted that involved sensation of the hand and a wet cloth. That is all I can recall. And that is precisely the problem – I cannot remember what I need to, including myself.

———————

At lunch in the small dining room at a workweek in San Francisco, I served Lord Pentland and some senior pupils lentil soup for lunch. He asked me what kind of soup it was when we were all seated. I said, "It's lentil soup, Lord Pentland." "This isn't lentil soup," he said. "Yes, it is," I replied. He then proceeded to ask each one of the pupils at that lunch what kind of soup it was. In spite of the fact that there were cooked lentils in their bowls, not one of them would say so, until the last person he asked did say, "I believe it is lentil soup, Lord Pentland." I was flabbergasted that no one would say what was true. Were they really that sheepish? Did they think this was only about him trying to teach me something and that it had nothing to do with them? I was beginning to understand that I did in fact innerly consider less than others.

We are told that a strong ego is needed in the work. To be a shrinking violet is not what the work needs. To be obedient for the sake of obedience serves nothing. To be consciously egoistic is in the right direction.

During a workweek, I am given the task of creating floral arrangements for the whole house. It was a team of two, the other person an older pupil who tended to be marginalized by others. I later learned that she suffered from severe anxiety, which increased my compassion for her. As I was out foraging for flowers one day, I returned to the site of our work to hear Lord Pentland say to my teammate, just before I rounded the corner, "She's difficult, you know." I knew that he was talking about me. The other person told Lord Pentland that she didn't find me so. But I don't mind being difficult at times. Where is the virtue in being easy for people? To be honest, I wouldn't have it any other way, as I have undertaken to be myself. I have come to understand myself as someone in whom "there is much good, and much bad." Perhaps then the struggles are more difficult or complex, but the possibilities for good are also prominent.

I remember that Gurdjieff had to pay the old Russian to step on others' toes at the Prieuré. Somebody's got to do it.

———————

As for being on the Fourth Way – a work in life as opposed to a monastic life – we are asked to take our work into life. I consider my vocation as a mental health therapist and counselor my life's work. I am profoundly grateful and fortunate to have a vocation I am well suited to – one that allows me to bring the work into it, one that requires my presence and attention.

# ON LOVE

My relationship with Lord Pentland was not all roses, but it was, I believe, based on a more conscious love than is common. I feel that of the hundreds of people who were touched deeply by him, many would say that they felt loved by him. As noted earlier, he said to me of love, "the wonderful thing about love is, you can give it, and give it, and give it, and there is always more to give." While we are cautioned about overestimating our ability to love, at a certain point, if one has really applied one's attention seriously to oneself, we can assess whether or not we are able to love. We can, as Lord Pentland said, "take our own measure."

One evening, I am visiting at a friend's house, and I am speaking negatively about Lord Pentland – this is how I am at that time, confused, and hurt. It is 10:30 p.m. The phone rings, and it is Lord Pentland. I have no idea how he knows that I am there, or what I am saying. He asks to speak directly to me and, as I get on the phone he says, "I love you, you know." I am chastened and ashamed.

On my birthday one year, Lord Pentland took me with his daughter, Mary, to the Four Seasons Restaurant for lunch to celebrate. It was a place I had mentioned wanting to go because I had heard that the strawberries there were amazing. It was here that Lord Pentland first spoke one of my favorite expressions of Gurdjieff: "If only people weren't people, but people are people." I'm not sure if I prefer that one best or "When it rains, the streets get wet."

---

I asked Paul Reynard about how Gurdjieff was with people, especially the severity that is documented in some accounts. He told me, on the contrary, that "Gurdjieff was loving." And, for what it's worth, a psychic acquaintance, who had never read *Beelzebub's Tales*, held the book in her hand and pronounced that Gurdjieff was all about love. And, when I think of the labor that was *Beelzebub's Tales*, I can think of no other reason he would write such a book other than a great love and compassion for humanity. For, although filled with data on cosmic history and physical laws that will, I believe, one day come to be verified as true, it is his abiding concern for humanity that shines through.

---

I am at the San Francisco Foundation for a workday and the secretary, Thelma Titus, comes to get me in the weaving shed. She says, "Lord Pentland says you must come immediately into the paneled room. Don't knock. Just go straight in." And I do. He is in the midst of severely dressing down a pupil, the most senior pupil. Just mercilessly hammering him. I stand there watching, stunned.

Years later, I mention this incident to the man in question, and he has no recollection of it. I say this not to disparage the man, because he was a man in whom there was much good, as well as much bad. I believe Lord Pentland wanted me to see, as he said, "I did the best I could with what I had." And that different methods are required for different pupils.

There is a story that is told in the theater community

about a legendary acting teacher who consistently asked his students to identify if a particular scene was a story about love or power, that it could only be one or the other. Apparently, on his deathbed, the acting teacher revised his understanding. "They are all love stories," he said. And so they are.

## WHAT IS THE NATURE OF IDENTIFICATION?

I asked in a group meeting in New York, "What is the nature of identification?" I see that Lord Pentland is interested in my question. It is not long before he shows me.

I am in a taxicab with Lord Pentland, Dick Brower, and one of Lord Pentland's main business contacts – a devastatingly charming Englishman. The gentleman, who may well have been hoping for a knighthood as Dick implied, is telling a story and showing us pictures of himself with Queen Elizabeth in the London Metro. His tone is reverential, almost obsequious. I, American through and through, say, "Really, she is a human being like the rest of us." I look at Lord Pentland. He is smiling at me, clearly amused by my impertinence.

Several times a year, visitors would come from the British companies and, if Lord Pentland was out of town, it fell to Dick Brower and me to entertain them. Dick, the Englishman, and I have dinner at the St. Regis in New York. There are violins, caviar, blini, and vodka, and the Englishman and I become infatuated. The prior, somewhat argumentative banter I previously shared with this man turns into its opposite.

Lord Pentland comes back from his trip and I am beside myself. I know that he will not be happy about this new development. Since we are working together all day, there are multiple moments for me to reveal what has happened, and I know I must tell him, but he doesn't give me a moment's opening. He is not letting me speak about it. Perhaps he wants me to suffer a while more, to "stay with the conflict longer," as he once exhorted me. It is agonizing, but he will not let me tell him. At the end of the second day of this, he sits down by my desk, observes me closely, and says, "Yes, you look very good," as if this suffering was good for me.

The next day, he permits me to tell him. He acts surprised, and is clearly angry, but not with me, with the businessman. I tell him that the man wants to take me to Rio, and we will live there. I assure him, though, that this will not happen. He disagrees: "Do not underestimate the man."

You understand, I needed a father. He took that on. And he was very angry with the man. In fact, I'd never seen him angry before that.

The next time the Englishman comes to New York, I am not permitted to come to the office. If I want to keep my job, Lord Pentland tells me, I must stay away. I leave the City and stay away for a few days. I am miserable. It feels as though there is a substance between this man and me, a palpable tar-like pull, even though he is miles away. I had always wondered what was the actual nature of identification. Now I knew. And I understood that identification has a molecular reality. That, as Gurdjieff said, "everything is material." And identification is sticky.

The next time the Englishman returns to New York, Lord Pentland says nothing, but the Englishman does not come to the office. Lord Pentland and Dick Brower are meeting with him elsewhere, surely by design. I say to God and to the powers that be, "If you want me to see this man, you will have to put him in my path." The workday ends, and I am heading for the Foundation. And who, among the hordes of people on Fifth Avenue at 5:00 p.m., do I run directly into but the Englishman? We make plans for an assignation later than evening, for the gods have ordained it.

I go to my group meeting at the Gurdjieff Foundation and tell Lord Pentland I would like to speak with him afterward. We go out for coffee after the meeting. Again, he will not let me broach the subject. He is brilliant at this. I am free to be with this man, it is clear to me, if that is what I wish to do. But the enchantment has been broken. I have seen the identification, and I wish to be free, not enslaved. I understand that this is not a good idea at all and that to carry this out would take me away from the Gurdjieff Work that I love so much. I go and have a lovely dinner with the man, and we part as friends.

L ord Pentland was and remains my foremost teacher. Even after I stopped attending the Foundation for a time, he told a friend, "Tell Jane I'm still her teacher." Lest I not grasp that fact, he made it explicit.

The relationship was characterized by love. And by love, I mean Lord Pentland *attended*. He once said in a group meeting, "What is love, if not attention?" And, as noted earlier "the wonderful thing about love is, you can give it and give it and give it, and there is always more to give." I am sure he was referring to that inexhaustible fount of love that is there is at the core of our being and the universe.

I am told by people who knew Lord Pentland when he was younger that he was rather severe. I was on the other side of that withering look a few times, and it was not pretty. I gather that he had a severe father, was a stutterer in his youth, and that may have been the reason. But as I knew him in his older age, I did not find that to be the case very often at all. I saw his actions as stemming from a deep attending.

———

I was sitting by his desk one day when he seemed to sneer and mentioned "hitting children. That is the way to handle them, to instill fear in them." I was appalled, and I told him, "I do not think that is right at all." I do not think he really believed that, I felt that he was processing something around that.

———————

Dick Brower (my coworker in the office) and I are out for cocktails at La Goulue, probably the most posh restaurant in NYC at the time. We are there with another close friend who was as devoted to the Work as a person could be. I made a pejorative statement about Lord Pentland. I said that I felt used by him. In fact he worked me very hard and my wages were low. He was Scots, after all. I hadn't had a vacation in I don't know how long. Dick and I had a huge blowout, and Dick had some choice, vulgar words for me. The friend who was there didn't say a word in my defense. Dick later struggled with Lord Pentland being human, but at the time he could only react negatively to me.

The next day I told Lord Pentland about it. I told him that he worked me too hard, and I needed a rest. He acknowledged that mistakes had been made. He gifted me a four-day cruise to the Caribbean. Let's just say that is four days I can never get back.

So I got vacations and I also asked for a raise, but for that I had to summon every ounce of strength in me in order to ask. "So, you want a rise," he said, dripping with challenge. But I got it!

Mistakes are made, but this is life on earth, this is how it is.

He gave me a week of vacation. I decided to head up to Maine by myself to a vacation spot I had some sentimentality about. There's no terrain I love more than lakes and conifers. I had planned to spend a week. A few days after getting there, I was sitting by the lake at a sublimely beautiful spot. I had just started to go negative about something when I heard the phone ring over the loud speaker. I knew it was Lord Pentland. I hear my name called over the loud speaker and pick up the phone,

"It's time to come home," he said to me.

When I talk to him about wanting a life of adventure and travel, he chastises me: "Don't you think I'd like to move to Banff?" (Note to self: Must get to Banff.)

———————

A friend from New York stayed in my home in San Francisco to attend a workweek that I was not attending. Early one morning when she is here, I am awakened by the sense that Lord Pentland is coming through my window, visiting with Love. This was at a particularly difficult period of my life, and I could have done with some love, the authentic kind. Later that evening, my friend tells me, "I was in the weaving shed this morning and Lord Pentland came through the door, walked straight to me, and said, 'Tell Jane I am sending her my love.'" He is teaching me to receive love.

## CHIEF FEATURE

I have a meeting with Lord Pentland in his room at the San Francisco Foundation on St. Elmo Way. It is the first time I have ever had a face-to-face meeting alone with him. He has a box of See's candy and offers me one, watching me closely the whole time I select and eat a piece. After I finish it, he says: "You don't wait long enough."

The next thing I know, I am walking down the street. With a shock, I realize that "I don't wait long enough." I leave too soon. I act too soon. I am too quick. I never stay long enough.

———————

There is a Movements demonstration at the New York Foundation. Mme. de Salzmann is there. Our class, that has performed, is sitting at the rear. I was in the front row, far left position, and at the start of the movement, I blundered ahead of the rest of the class by a fraction of a second.

Afterward, Mme. de Salzmann is talking to the whole group of dancers. She is sitting about thirty feet away. Suddenly she is looking at me and I hear her saying, in my chest, "You cannot be even a fraction of a second too early." She is too far away from me for me to hear, she is speaking in another octave of communication. It is reminiscent of Ouspensky hearing Gurdjieff speak inside of him in Tiflis. And there it is again. I just couldn't wait another second to start. I just had to go.

The next day, Lord Pentland tells me, "I suppose I should tell you that you did well last night." I didn't tell him what Mme. de Salzmann said to me, but I should have, for I am certain he saw the same thing.

---

I am in the office at Rockefeller Plaza and Lord Pentland calls from the West Coast. "What is different about you?" he asks.

I tell him I saw that if I keep getting everything done as quickly and efficiently as I do, I will have lived my whole life being efficient, and barely lived. Everything would have gotten done, but what would have been truly accomplished? And that realization slowed me down.

---

The chief feature is what we call in psychology an organizing principle. It is that around which one's psyche revolves. It develops according to type and conditioning in our early years and it results in a pervasive personality trait or adaptation. It works both for and against a person. It helps and hinders. It is the proverbial stick with two ends. And it is within our ken to know it. I have a theory that Lord Pentland told people his or her chief feature. Maybe he didn't name it as such, but he indicated it.

Let us posit that I am too quick or very quick. I leave bad situations quickly, I can sense danger for example, and move away from it. I can also seize an opportunity. I'm a fairly quick study. On the opposing end of the stick, I don't stay long enough, I am skittish. I miss out on good things, relationships, for example, because I cannot stay "long enough," as Lord Pentland told me. It started early. If I leave quickly, no one will be able to get to me. If I leave completely, I am safe. If I leave, I can't be hurt.

An interesting, and terrifying, example of this was on a drive cross-country with some friends in 1970. Outside of Los Angeles in the desert, we are hailed over by the driver of a psychedelically painted bus. We stop because it is the summer of Love and there is a party everywhere. I am first to enter the bus. I look into the eyes of the man in the bus driver's seat and see nothing but pure evil. I turn to my friends and say, "Run!"

Months later, the face of Charles Manson is plastered all over the newspapers, and it is the face of the man I encountered on that bus. My chief feature, my prematurity, in that case, perchance saved our lives.

———————

Here is a story about the great Hassid teacher, Rabbi Ben Asher, concerning subjectivity. It is told that the great rabbi was on his deathbed when he was suddenly astonished by something he'd seen. He turned to his chief disciple and said to him, "I have spent my whole life preparing to answer a question I believed God was going to ask me at the end of my life. And I see now that the question I was preparing to answer was incorrect." The disciple asked him, "What was the question you spent your whole life preparing to answer?" And the rabbi said, "I spent my whole life preparing to answer this that I thought God was going to ask me, 'Why were you not more like Moses, the great leader of your people?'" And the disciple then asked, "What, then, is the question that God is going to ask you?" And Rabbi Ben Asher replied, "Why were you not more like Rabbi Ben Asher?" So much for trying to be other than who we are.

## IT IS A BLESSING TO BE BORN INTO A BLOODLINE
## WHERE THERE ARE THINGS TO BE WORKED OUT

I was happily thunderstruck when I heard this read from a previously unpublished talk of Gurdjieff's. It spoke to what I felt about my own experience within my family, that maybe I was the only one who had any interest in understanding the dynamics of it, in working through the dysfunction and not passing it on to future generations.

It was also affirming when I read that Gurdjieff's intent was for his teaching to return people to the religion of their birth. This I also felt was not accidental, even with as much difficulty as I have understanding the strictures of religion and dogma. It was the same I felt when in movements we were asked to speak "Mother" or "Father." Or told that we had to go as far back as our grandfather or grandmother. The same feeling that this was a right direction came when I read of Gurdjieff's exercise for people to tell their life stories to the group.

We have mothers and fathers, and trauma, and conditions of difficulty and suffering. We have the possibility of being not saints, but ourselves.

We have a real possibility of transformation, for if we actually do the work on ourselves we will suffer consciously and turn ourselves upside down, like the Hanged Man in the Tarot deck.

As meditators learn, you cannot reject the sounds outside, they are not a distraction, they are life itself, and sound is miraculous. That we are here at all is miraculous. Similarly, we are not to reject parts of ourselves. Our sorrows are given to us, they are admixed with our daily bread. We are called to unify the parts of ourselves through our awareness; to become as one.

Gurdjieff tells us that our hope is in "conscious labor and intentional suffering." What can this possibly mean other than to take on our suffering consciously? Instead, we reject our sorrow, we have misbegotten ideas about not suffering. We think we should be happy. Even the Dalai Lama, who generally seems quite joyful, when queried by an interviewer about his meditation, confessed to struggling with anger and jealousy every day in his meditation. There is no use idealizing these people, and make ourselves small in relation to them. Our struggles are the same, or similar. What does the Dalai Lama have to be angry about? They took his country and tried to take his religion away. And jealousy, I cannot imagine who he might be jealous of. People who have children? Spouses? The point is, he shows us his humanity.

Lord Pentland said, I believe at a public meeting: "The difference between me and you, is that I have negative emotions, only I don't feel bad about them."

Gurdjieff, in some of the movements he gave, had people speak the words "Mother" and "Father." There is something in this. It is not to sanctify our parents, but to know where we came from, how we were conditioned, and to work through the difficulties. And bless the source of our arising. We have a divine part, a spark, a higher consciousness is available to us, distinct and separate from the ego. But I need to study myself, all of myself.

From the first reading of Gurdjieff's teaching, as exposited by Ouspensky in *In Search of the Miraculous*, it was obvious that Gurdjieff cared as much about our possibility of coming into relationship with what is higher as he cared about our harmonious *psychological* development. This division into two domains speaks to our two natures, to the Above and Below of us. An over-emphasis on one or the other aspect will foster a lopsided development.

Furthermore, I was able to observe that, as I worked with my psyche – the neuroses, the complexes, the sorrow and grief – my capacity to experience what was Higher in me, and to have a more conscious contact with that, was proportionately increased.

# DULY CHASTENED

We are at a workweek in upstate New York. Lord Pentland asks one of the other elders how she would feel if she was trying to explain something to a student and the student didn't understand. She said that she would think the other person had limits to their understanding. Lord Pentland said that he would feel that he had failed to explain himself properly. I think that he was trying to tell this woman something about herself. In any case, I think of this often, and how, in my work, if someone does not understand something, I keep trying, until I find a way to describe the thing I am trying to explain.

------------

Minor White, the great photographer, is visiting at the workhouse in upstate New York. He is asked a question and, in his response, I detect a judgment, a kind of contempt even, toward the student asking it. Lord Pentland asks me the next day what I thought about the lunch discussion. I share my impression with him. He chastises me, "Don't you think he saw that about himself?"

------------

When I tell him I'd spent some time with one of his favorite pupils, he says, "Now you're part of the inner circle," as he rotates around himself. I am ashamed of my shallowness, my need to assert my ego with him.

———————

Lord Pentland had business in many third world countries, and something had to be delivered to the Ugandan Embassy. Idi Amin was then in power. He insisted that both Dick Brower and I go to the Ugandan Embassy. There was so much chaos in that embassy, I began to think it must really be crazy in Uganda. Lord Pentland was generous in wanting his students to have many impressions, impressions on many levels, of life and of themselves.

———————

Lord Pentland was looking for an office as it was time to move out of Rockefeller Plaza, closer to the Foundation. I was not happy about the move. He asked me one day, "How would you like to work in the World Trade Center?" I shuddered and said, "I would not like it one bit." I don't for a moment think he was considering moving his office there. I simply do not understand the need to build towering skyscrapers. It feels unnatural to me, out of a Divine Blueprint I imagine exists. They feel like Towers of Babel. It is horrible what happened there, of course.

———————

I bring up the question of whether his business is exploiting third world countries, a typical liberal point of view. And he chides me, "On the contrary, we are bringing money and jobs to places that need it." I actually hadn't thought of that, so I appreciated his point of view. I believe he tended to be conservative politically, no doubt attributable to his aristocratic upbringing. Dick Brower told me that Lord Pentland had met every living United States president.

---

I observed that when I approached a man we both knew that the man jumped a bit when I approached him. Lord Pentland said, "That's his problem, not yours."

---

In a meeting he tells me, in front of others, "You, above all, need to learn when to talk and when to remain silent."

---

Someone's wife and small child have been killed in a car accident and Lord Pentland has asked me to go upstate New York and take care of the widowed man. It is obviously a tragic situation, but I feel vulnerable and frightened, even superstitious. I am young, and it is too much for me. Crying, I tell him I cannot go. "I need you to be strong," he demands. But I refuse to go.

---

I tell him I feel safe in the work. He tells me that it was even more so of a feeling that nothing could touch you when you were around Gurdjieff.

---

Lord Pentland tells me that when he first moved to New York City he walked every street, from the bottom of Manhattan to the top.

———————

He tells me that his favorite natural symbol is the tree. He asks me what mine is, and I tell him that it is the heavens.

Lord Pentland went on many journeys with people and I hope some of them will someday soon recount their own tales.

Lord Pentland, Dick Brower, Dianne Edwards and I are going to the Jersey Shore for a picnic on the weekend. The day before we go he asks me how to get to the Jersey Shore. Mind you, I had never been to the Jersey Shore nor had I ever driven a car, yet I was only too willing to give directions to get there. He interrupts me, "Why are you talking about something you know nothing about?"

———————

I was never fond of airplane travel. Lord Pentland clearly observed this and would help me by talking to me while we were flying. As well, he gave me candy to distribute to people on the airplane. He was showing me that I needed to keep busy, and not indulge my fear.

———————

Lord Pentland has invited me to travel to San Francisco for a workweek there. At some point, he gives me the day off. On my day off, he asks me what I will be doing. I tell him that I am going to visit various people at their workplaces. He tells me "It is a good thing that you are interested in people."

———————

Later, after I have moved back to California, he asks me to come to Marin County to type something. I was, for better or worse, an inveterate talker, and there are plenty of people there to speak with, so nothing is getting typed. In frustration with me, he moves the typewriter and me into his bedroom, where no one will go. He then goes out to sail on a single small rig. I watch him as he sails out into the lagoon. And then I see him fall off into the water.

He comes into the room, dripping water. "I didn't forget myself, not even for a second," he says to me, with a big grin on his face.

# SHAMANISM/DREAMTIME

Lord Pentland told me once that Gurdjieff said "Women make the best shamans." I felt naturally that he was inviting me to look into shamanism.

Shamanism posits, among other things, that we are in concordance with nature, or at least we have the possibility of being so, though we may be alienating ourselves from the beautiful and good graces of the living Earth.

I have had several encounters with animals, for example, that suggest we are deeply entwined with nature.

I have packed up my two very small children to leave my home in the Santa Cruz Mountains in California. I am moving the three of us to San Francisco to start a new life. As I am driving down the winding mountain road, I become aware that a cougar has taken a running jump from a rise on my right, over my vehicle, to the other side of the road. While it is terrifying, I know that it signals something. Later, when I begin to study the iconography of animal totems, I discover that cougar symbolizes coming into one's power, especially feminine power.

Then again, in the mountains of upstate New York, I am with friends and I have the strongest feeling that God – however that may be understood – will soon appear, and I tell my friends this. Within minutes, a magnificent stag and two smaller deer appear just across the stream from where we are sitting. We have a quiet "meeting" with them.

———

My mother died this year, having lived to the very ripe age of 95. A couple of hours after she died, outside my office window came a display of birds, different kinds of birds – finches, hummingbirds, blue birds, and more – swooping and dipping. I've been in this office over nine years and have never seen so many birds show up at one time. I have read about this – displays of birds or butterflies showing up at a person's death.

And then, of course, the Cooper's Hawk shows up outside my window as I began to write this book and stays for a while.

A friend has told me that Lord Pentland told her and others to study the birds that show up in their lives.

———————

Another way of contact with ourselves of a deeper type is through dreaming. Though many dreams are obviously mundane in nature, others can connect us to collective events or our Higher Self. I can give some credence to the idea that we leave our corporeal bodies at night based on the following.

I used to dream often of my childhood home, but the last time, a few years ago, it had an unsightly chain link fence around it. This was very odd as the house was beautiful and a fence, definitely not a chain link one, did not befit it. I tell this to a friend of mine who suggests we look at the house on Google Earth, something at the time I did not even know existed. He finds the house that was 3,000 miles away in New York, a house I hadn't seen in 30 years, and it was indeed surrounded by a chain link fence.

———————

Three weeks before Lord Pentland died, I had a dream in which he gave me certain information that was comforting to me and that in due course turned out to be true. Among other things, he told me that it was all right that my children be taught the religious fundamentalism of their father and that they would be none the worse for it.

My son at 11 years old wakes and tells me that, in the night, he visited the seven realms of the universe and learned of the different teachings therein. He tells me what they are in detail. There is no way he had ever been exposed to ideas of this nature. Further, as a teenager, he sees an Indian chief standing in full dress, including a headdress, on the banks of the Russian River days before it floods. Looking back again, he sees that he is not there any longer.

It does seem that our consciousness is moveable and not inextricably linked with our physical bodies.

## ON THE INSTITUTIONALIZATION OF THE
## WORK/HIERARCHY, HIEROPHANTS, HIEROPHANT-ASSES

I quoted Lord Pentland as asking me to "study the institutionalization of the Work." I think he had multiple reasons for telling me that. He knew that my own tendency or chief feature, as it were, to leave too early, would inevitably be expressed in my relationship to the Gurdjieff Foundation. I believe his thinking was that if I could study the institutionalization, I would be less likely to react emotionally to it. Alas, I could not stay on much beyond his death. In any case, my work in life with other people as a therapist has enabled me to spread the ideas in a practical manner and is, I believe, helping to alleviate at least some small amount of human suffering. I feel that I have been of much more use in my profession than I ever would have been as part of any Foundation.

It is, of course, lawful that a body of thought becomes institutionalized. Studying the history of any religion will verify this. Some truths remain naturally cogent over time, while others, obviously, lose their freshness, or even become bastardized. Witness religious fundamentalism of all stripes, where the original teacher invariably taught impartiality, conscious love, and freedom from judgment and witness the devolution of some religions into judgment and platitude.

I asked Lord Pentland this: "Why do we have the same meeting week after week, at the same time, year after year? Would Gurdjieff have wanted that?" It was then he told me that Gurdjieff asked him to "set up a Foundation, with an office, and have meetings." Being mutable by nature, I didn't love the idea of doing the same thing year after year. Perhaps this was a task specifically for Lord Pentland and certainly it has provided beneficial conditions for many people. But for me, the handwriting was on the wall, and I stopped attending the Foundations several years after Lord Pentland died.

This does not mean that I "left the Work" in the parlance of modern-day acolytes. One can never leave the "Work" unless one elects unconsciousness as a path. Indeed, the Work exists anywhere and everywhere, by different names, or no names.

In *Beelzebub's Tales,* Gurdjieff implies that every being is on a path to God. The Work, a Work, is a way that puts a being on a more accelerated path toward the Absolute. Some routes are accelerated, and some may take much, much longer, but it is inevitable that we find our way home.

———————

I once felt that I had understood that the problems I saw within the Institution were actually problems that I had within myself. I had thought that was especially perspicacious. I brought it to Lord Pentland. "No," he said, "not all of what you see as problems with the Work are reflective of your own problems. *The Work has problems of its own.*" The Work is not a perfect place. That is not its point. But it is a cauldron and it cooks up some very good conditions.

———————

I think that the groups are excellent for several things: (1) the teaching and practice of the work with attention, through which many wondrous things become possible; (2) the conduction of the energy of the Higher into the human being who is prepared to receive it, bear it, and thus change the world through her or his emanations, and (3) the teaching and practice of the Sacred Dances or Movements, which transmit esoteric teachings symbolically. As well, the brushing up against types one might not normally consort with is conducive to the psychological work of bearing the unpleasant manifestations of others toward oneself. I hope that this present exposition will encourage a new wave of study of Gurdjieff's ideas with regard to the psychology he puts forth.

----

I come now to the subject of prophets and kings. One must not confuse the kings, or administrators, with the prophets. Kings/administrators are necessary to keep a thing afloat, to preserve, to archive, and to plan. But they are not necessarily prophets. The prophets are the ones that sound and embody the notes of truth. They may be found anywhere. And that may shift, for in one moment one may embody something prophetic and truthful, and the next moment be utterly asleep.

I quote Lord Pentland again from the interview he gave nine months before he died (*Telos, The Gurdjieff Journal,* Volume 1, Issue 7).

> Often the people who are best at organizing
> a community or school, and who are best at
> making limitations [rules], the sensible

ones, are not those who are most serious in
their search.

And,

Usually, the ones who are most sincere in
their inner search are rather invisible to the
public because they sometimes avoid
positions of outer responsibility.

With regard to these charming power-possessors, one
of the elders in San Francisco had the temerity to tell me that
he "didn't know what Lord Pentland was trying to do with me."
And I said right back to him, "And I have no idea what he was
trying to do with you either."

---

As he was leaving his own Group One meeting one day, Lord
Pentland turned to me in a hallway and said: "Hierarchy,
Heirophants, Heirophant-asses!"

Gurdjieff decried the way human beings relate to one
another: always measuring who is above, or who is below, not
striving to be equal to. This way of relating to people is an example
of the institutionalization. It is not fully alive, or true, or good.

I complain to Lord Pentland one day that people are
"identified with the Work." He tells me, "It's not your problem."
And, indeed, it was not. I was neither overly identified with the
Work, nor did I ever wish for and actively resisted being in an
administrative position or group leader, consequently other people's
identifications were not my problem. I knew I had another path.

When I first met Michel de Salzmann in Lord Pentland's office, he asked me if I liked working for Lord Pentland. I told him that I aspired to something greater, that I did not want to be somebody's assistant (I realize that this is ironic). I was obviously very young and did not recognize the extraordinary gift I had been given. M. de Salzmann said this to me then, "No matter where you go in the universe, you will always be of service to something."

Lord Pentland tells me that M. de Salzmann was interested in me, and that "he can tell a person of quality." I take in what he is telling me, but it takes me years to grasp that I am worth the teaching, worth loving, and worth being. We all are.

———————

Gurdjieff tells us that Life itself is the great teacher. I have certainly been able to verify that. The very things I once considered obstacles, I now see are necessary to promote individual development. Apparent obstacles actually provide the opportunity to evolve ourselves and, moreover, to help others.

Furthermore, we are told that this is a work of self-initiation. That is, *intermediaries are not needed.* Teachers are most helpful along the way, but it is we who invite ourselves into the Great Mystery.

———————

We are also told that this is a preparatory school. This is almost never spoken about, because what, in fact, do we know of it?

I believe that the real school comes later, after we leave our corporeal bodies.

## BEHIND ME

Lord Pentland has invited me to a rehearsal of a movements demonstration in San Francisco. I am sitting by myself in the large, empty auditorium when he enters accompanied by someone. He observes the room and comes and sits directly behind me. He has problems with his health, with his heart. I wonder how he is. I wish for him.

Again, I am at a wedding of good friends, waiting for the ceremony to begin. Lord Pentland enters, observes the crowd and, winding his way, stands directly behind me.

Later, after the wedding ceremony, he finds me and tells me two things. "Take responsibility for what you know," he says. And, "You should help people. Probably you are already doing this, helping people." These are tall orders that I do not take lightly. Every day in my work I ponder what it is that might help this person in front of me. It is not necessarily obvious, and it most certainly is not telling people what to do or giving advice.

———————

Many a time in my life I have failed to take full responsibility for what I know. I am engaged in a struggle best described by Gurdjieff this way, "The whole of an adult's life should be a struggle between yes and no." This statement of Gurdjieff's gives dignity to the struggle of human beings to be good, to have some mastery over one's unruly appetites, "to gird the loins of one's mind," as Lord Pentland put it. I know I *should* do this, but *it* wants to do something else.

It is the struggle that counts. Struggle is our domain. But being human, we cannot expect complete victory. In the words of Moses Maimonides, "It is not possible to complete the work, but neither are we at liberty to not take it up."

We live in a culture that extols material success and egoism and thus is fostered and maintained the life of the ego. But of those who struggle with being human and all that entails, quite apart from worldly success, it is said, "And the meek shall inherit the earth."

———————

"Never underestimate the resistance," Lord Pentland says. One day, I see that I resist everything. I have a problem with everything. The resistance is in my body and mind. I say no to everything. I want life to be different than it is. Later on, I begin to relax into life, little by little, and I learn that the difficulties of life, my life, have their own teachings. I no longer fight with life. As Gurdjieff said, "Life is the great teacher."

———————

People have asked me to write this. I feel a responsibility to pass on what I was given. As I sit down in earnest to begin the writing, and make a prayer for its success, an enormous bird flies into the palm tree directly outside my office window. I have never seen such a large bird as close as this one is. I go downstairs and outside to see it and we make eye contact for quite a while, half an hour. I take many pictures. It is a Cooper's Hawk. In the iconography of sacred animal totems, the hawk is a messenger. I've seen many birds outside my window – but none this commanding.

I have fulfilled a number of tasks in this life. But this one – the passing on of the gifts I have received from Lord Pentland – feels deeply important.

———————

After I have stopped working for him, Lord Pentland calls and invites me to lunch at the Ritz-Carlton. We talk of many things. I tell him that I wish for him to be free of the psoriasis that has afflicted him. I can see that this touches him. We go outside to say our goodbyes. He is very tall, and I am very small. He reaches down toward me. And he lifts me up.

# EPILOGUE

I remember exactly where we were standing when, at the end of a long day in the office, I said to Lord Pentland, "Thank you. Thank you for everything." He replied, "Thank you." We then went a few rounds thanking one another, which was serious and playful at the same time. The exchange ended when he said to me, "Don't thank me now. You will thank me later."

I also remember the time when I thanked him for bearing me, and he then thanked me for bearing him. He was not easy to bear. So that made two of us.

---

After he died, someone I'd never spoken with approached me. She told me that Lord Pentland told her he was proud of the way I turned out. And I was not doing that well at the time he said that.

I do feel that he was able to right the path I was on so that I would have not only a decent life, but that I would come to know something finer. As well, he taught me at least how to approximate the right kind of Self-Love. I believe I learned about loving from him, that which I had not learned in my family of origin. It is impossible to imagine what my life would have been like without Lord Pentland or Gurdjieff informing it. And I am in awe of the luck that brought me along in this way.

I have learned that I must act in accordance with my own conscience. And thus have I written this account.

I know that there will be all kinds of responses to this tale. My perspective is that if I have helped one or two people get through a rough night that it was well worth the effort.

At the very least, I hope this small work will encourage Lord Pentland's students to reflect on the lessons they learned from him and that some will be willing to share their good news with the rest of us.

Lord Pentland was devoted to loving – to helping – all of us. There was no other reason that he did this for us. We are still profiting from his efforts, what he built.

Lord Pentland said to one of my friends, "I built this." I asked him recently what that meant to him, because for years I thought he had meant that he had built the Work, the groups, St. Elmo. My friend tells me that he felt Lord Pentland meant that he created himself, that he was a result of his own efforts. That interpretation offers hope to all of us.

He gave so much, and enriched so many lives. I cannot believe our great good fortune.

And to Lord Pentland: It is now "later." And I thank you with all of the being that I have and am.

# ACKNOWLEDGMENTS

I am deeply grateful to my friend Roger Lipsey, who has mentored this project with wisdom, kindness and patience. Plainly said, his guidance was invaluable.

As well, I am so grateful for the ongoing encouragement and feedback of Gretchen Gold (no relation) and Barbara Hart in seeing this work and me through to its publication, and for the aesthetic skill and friendship of Mark Dolin, who saw me through the final stages of this book.

Bob Scher, piano man extraordinaire, thank you for the title of this book. You are missed.

And to the others, friends and helpers all, simply thank you for your presence and your work.

And for my children and grandchildren, Aaron Tomforde, Anna and Nathan Collins, Gabriel Tomforde, Mia and Levi Collins, you are the lights of my life, and you have made my sojourn here very, very beautiful.

# BIBLIOGRAPHY/READING LIST

*Autobiography of a Yogi*, Paramahansa Yogananda

*Awakening the Sacred Body*, Tenzin Wangyal Rinpoche

*Beelzebub's Tales to His Grandson, All and Everything, or An Objectively Impartial Criticism of the Life of Man*, First Series, George Ivanovich Gurdjieff

*Conference of the Birds*, Farid Ud-din Attar

*Cosmic Consciousness: A Study in the Evolution of the Human Mind*, Richard Maurice Bucke

*Drama of the Gifted Child, or Prisoners of Childhood*, Alice Miller

*Final Gifts: Understanding the Special Awareness, Needs and Communications of the Dying*, Maggie Callanan and Patricia Kelley

*Gurdjieff, A Master in Life*, Tcheslaw Tchekhovitch

*Gurdjieff Reconsidered. The Life, the Teachings, the Legacy*, Roger Lipsey

*I Am That*, Nisargadatta Maharaj

*Inner Yoga*, Sri Anirvan

*In Search of the Miraculous, Fragments of an Unknown Teaching*, P. D. Ouspensky

*Meetings with Remarkable Men, All and Everything*, Second Series, G. I. Gurdjieff

*Life is Real Only Then, When "I Am," All and Everything*, Third Series, G.I. Gurdjieff

*The New Man*, Maurice Nicoll

*On Love & Psychological Exercises*, A. R. Orage

*On the Way to Self-Knowledge*, Jacob Needleman & Dennis Lewis

*Parabola*, Vol. 38, No. 2: The Night I Died, Tracy Cochran

*Periphyseon: On the Division of Nature*, John the Scot

*Psychological Commentaries on the Teaching of Gurdjieff & Ouspensky*, Vols. 1 through 5, Maurice Nicoll

*Reality of Being*, Jeanne de Salzmann

*Sword of Gnosis: Metaphysics, Cosmology, Tradition, Symbolism*, Jacob Needleman

*Telos (The Gurdjieff Journal)*, Volume 1, Issue 7, Interview: Lord John Pentland

*To Live Within*, Lizelle Reymond & Sri Anirvan

*Transitional Man: the anatomy of a miracle*, Franklin Earnest III

*Views from the Real World: Early Talks*, G.I. Gurdjieff

*Wonders of the Natural Mind*, Tenzin Wangyal Rinpoche

*Lord Pentland and George Gurdjieff.*

CPSIA information can be obtained
at www.ICGtesting.com
Printed in the USA
BVHW030012160721
612045BV00007B/290